Essential
Tuscany
&
Florence

by Tim Jepson

PASSPORT BOOKS

NTC/Contemporary Publishing Company

Published by Passport Books, an imprint of NTC/
Contemporary Publishing Company, 4255 West Touhy
Avenue, Lincolnwood (Chicago), Illinois 60646–1975 U.S.A.

Above: *Peaceful Tuscan
landscape near Monte
Amiata*

Page 1: The *Campanile
high above Florence*

Page 5a: *Fiesole,
Florence*
5b: *Parked scooters in
Florence*

Page15a: *Pisa's Leaning
Tower*
15b: *Michelangelo's*
David

Page 27a: *Pisa*
27b: *Baptistry Door,
Florence*

Page 91a: *Ferrari Daytona*
91b: *Postcard buying in
Florence*

Page 117a: *Florentine
marbled paper*
117b: Carabinieri, *Piazza
della Signoria*

The contents of this publication are believed correct at
the time of printing. Nevertheless, the publishers cannot
accept responsibility for errors or omissions, nor for
changes in details given. We are always grateful to
readers who let us know of any errors or omissions
they come across, and future printings will be updated
accordingly.

Published by Passport Books in conjunction with
The Automobile Association of Great Britain.

Written by Tim Jepson

Library of Congress Catalog Card Number: on file
ISBN 0–8442–0123–5

Color separation: BTB Digital Imaging, Whitchurch,
Hampshire

Printed and bound in Italy by Printer Trento srl

The weather chart on **page 118** of this book is
calibrated in °C. For conversion to °F simply use the
following formula:

$$°F = 1.8 \times °C + 32$$

Contents

About this Book

Essential *Tuscany & Florence* is divided into five sections to cover the most important aspects of your visit to Tuscany and Florence.

Viewing Tuscany & Florence pages 5–14
An introduction to Tuscany and Florence by the author.
    Features of Tuscany and Florence
    Essence of Tuscany and Florence
    The Shaping of Tuscany and Florence
    Peace and Quiet
    Famous of Tuscany and Florence

Top Ten pages 15–26
The author's choice of the Top Ten places to see in Tuscany and Florence, each with practical information.

What to See pages 27–90
The main areas of Florence and Tuscany, each with its own brief introduction and an alphabetical listing of the main attractions.
    Practical information
    Snippets of 'Did You Know…' information
    2 suggested walks
    2 suggested tours
    2 features

Where To… pages 91–116
Detailed listings of the best places to eat, stay, shop, take the children and be entertained.

Practical Matters pages 117–24
A highly visual section containing essential travel information.

Maps
All map references are to the individual maps found in the What to See section of this guide.
For example, Ponte Vecchio has the reference ➕ 28C2 – indicating the page on which the map is located and the grid square in which the bridge is to be found. A list of all the maps that have been used in this travel guide can be found in the index.

Prices
Where appropriate, an indication of the cost of an establishment is given by **£** signs:
£££ denotes higher prices, **££** denotes average prices, while **£** denotes lower charges.

Star Ratings
Most of the places described in this book have been given a separate rating:

✪✪✪   Do not miss
✪✪   Highly recommended
✪   Worth seeing

Viewing
Tuscany &
Florence

Tim Jepson's Tuscany & Florence

Essential Florence
Baptistery: mosaics and doors
Campanile: general view
Cappella Brancacci: fresco cycle
Cappelle Medicee: Michelangelo sculptures
Duomo: view from the dome
Palazzo Medici-Riccardi: Gozzoli fresco cycle
Palazzo Pitti: paintings
Michelangelo's *David*
Santa Croce: tombs and frescoes
Santa Maria Novella: Masaccio's *Trinità* and fresco cycles
Uffizi: paintings

Essential Tuscany
Arezzo: San Francesco (frescoes of Piero della Francesca)
Cortona: Museo Diocesano (Fra Angelico paintings)
Lucca: Duomo, San Michele, walls and town
Monte Oliveto Maggiore: Sodoma and Signorelli frescoes
Pienza: Duomo, village
Pisa: Leaning Tower, Duomo and Baptistery
San Gimignano: Collegiata and village
Siena: Campo, Duomo, Ospedale, Museo dell'Opera, Pinacoteca and Palazzo Pubblico

Imagine you had to pick just one city to represent all that humankind has achieved. You would be hard pushed to improve on Florence, whose churches, museums and galleries contain some of the greatest works of art ever produced. Imagine, then, that you had to choose a landscape in which to live for ever, one of whose beauty and endless variety you would never tire. You might happily plump for Tuscany, whose bucolic countryside has been fashioned by chance and centuries of toil into a glorious and almost perfect scenic patchwork.

Florence is not entirely devoted to art, however, and visitors who restrict themselves to paintings and sculpture will come away with memories of a forbidding indoor city. It's essential to leave the rather gloomy streets and brooding palaces for the city's gardens, bridges and half-hidden corners, and still more vital to join the Florentines – some of the most chic of all Italians – in their pursuit of outdoor pleasures, whether it's window-shopping in Via dei Tornabuoni or sipping drinks in the city's elegant, old-world cafés.

In Tuscany the choice of pleasure is greater still, from cities with a wide array of culture – notably Siena and Lucca – to the endless possibilities of the region's beautiful countryside. There are hills, mountains and sandy beaches, and a hundred village squares lined with rustic trattorias and bustling bars. And not so far from the beaten track lie towns such as Pienza, Cortona and San Gimignano, each a perfect combination of the culture, charm and beauty which make this unusually favoured region so irresistible.

An archetypal Tuscan landscape, complete with cypresses

Features of Tuscany & Florence

Geography
- Latitude of Florence: 43° 46 minutes north – the same as Toronto (Canada) and Sapporo (Japan)
- Longitude of Florence: 11° 14 minutes east
- Area of Tuscany: 22, 992 sq km
- Altitude of Florence: 49m above sea level
- Height of Duomo: 91m
- Highest point in Tuscany: Monte Cimone (2,165m)
- Most densely wooded region in Italy: Tuscany
- Length of the River Arno in Tuscany: 241km

Climate
- Average January temperature: 6°C
- Average August temperature: 25°C
- Average October rainfall: 12.4cm
- Average July rainfall: 3.5cm
- Average annual rainfall: 89.4cm
- Height above street level of 1966 flood: 6m

Degrees of Wealth
In the 15th century an average family could live comfortably on 150 florins a year (the florin was the standard Florentine currency). A palace could be bought for 1,000 florins, a Botticelli painting for 100, a slave for 50 and a servant for 10. To give some idea of the ruling Medici family's wealth, their account books for the years 1433–71 showed 663,755 florins spent over 38 years simply on 'buildings, charitie and taxes'.

People
- Population of Florence in June 1996: 381,762
- Population in June 1995: 385,969
- Population in June 1994: 388,969
- Population of Tuscany: 3.5 million

Crowds of visitors congregating on the Ponte Vecchio

Tourism
- Annual number of visitors to Florence: 7 million (estimate)
- Most popular museum and gallery: Galleria degli Uffizi
- Annual number of visitors to the Uffizi: 1,150,093 (1995)

Essence of Tuscany & Florence

Florence seduces with its art and culture, Tuscany with its hill-towns and timeless scenery. Europe's greatest Renaissance paintings and sculptures crowd the city's churches and galleries, while ancient vineyards, gnarled olives and cypress-topped hills make up one of Italy's most beautiful regional landscapes. Beyond the lures of culture and countryside, however, lie more subtle charms: the simple pleasures of a hazy-hilled view, for example; or the best ice-creams and tastiest cappuccinos in Europe; bustling bars and pavement cafés; dining under the stars, or a stroll around geranium-hung streets on a summer evening.

THE 10 ESSENTIALS

If you only have a short time to visit Tuscany & Florence, or would like to get a really complete picture of the region, here are the essentials:

- **See Michelangelo's *David*** – so familiar it's a cliché, but something you still have to see (▶ 19).
- **Climb the Campanile** – struggle up the stairs for a breathtaking view of Florence (▶ 33). Alternatively, climb to the top of the cathedral dome for a similar panorama (▶ 37).
- **See the top museums** – you can't escape the art: be sure to visit the Uffizi for the paintings (▶ 26), the Bargello for the sculpture (▶ 22).

- **Take an evening stroll** – head for the Arno bridges, and the Ponte Vecchio in particular, for some of Florence's most romantic night-time views (▶ 52).
- **Sip a drink in the Campo** – treat yourself to a drink in a café on Siena's Piazza del Campo, one of Italy's most beautiful medieval squares (▶ 16).
- **Enjoy an *al fresco* lunch** – eating out is one of Tuscany's greatest pleasures: find a restaurant with outside tables and

Above: *A peaceful moment on the River Arno at Pisa*

Left: *The Giardino di Boboli are Italy's most visited gardens (left)*

- **Walk in the Boboli Gardens** – 5 million visitors a year can't be wrong: take a break from sightseeing in Italy's most visited gardens (▶ 38).
- **Eat an ice-cream** – buy an ice-cream from *Vivoli*, widely considered to be one of Italy's best *gelaterie*, and eat it sitting in nearby Piazza Santa Croce (▶ 57).
- **Visit Santa Croce** – Tuscany's greats are buried in this church, among them Michelangelo, Galileo and Machiavelli. As an added attraction there are frescoes by Giotto and other medieval artists (▶ 24).

forget the sightseeing in favour of a leisurely lunch (▶ 56 and 96–101).
- **Visit San Gimignano** – the village to see in Tuscany if you see no other, known as the 'medieval Manhattan' for its crop of ancient towers (▶ 80–2).

Below: *Santa Croce rises majestically above Florence's rooftops*

The Shaping of Tuscany & Florence

800 BC
First evidence of the Etruscans in Tuscany.

500 BC
Etruscan expansion and the growth of an Etruscan colony at Fiesole in the hills above Florence.

205 BC
The Romans establish control over Tuscany and exact tributes from the Etruscans.

59 BC
Florence (*Florentia*) is founded as colony for retired army veterans, following laws promulgated by Julius Caesar.

20 BC
Siena (*Saena*) is founded as a Roman military outpost.

AD 250
Eastern monks and merchants bring Christianity to Florence.

552
Totila the Goth and a barbarian army attack Florence.

An Etruscan plate, among Tuscany's earliest artefacts

570
The Lombards conquer much of northern Italy and establish a base in Lucca.

800
Charlemagne defeats the Lombards and is crowned Holy Roman Emperor. Tuscany is ruled from Lucca by imperial princes known as Margraves.

1115
Matilda, the last Margrave, bequeaths her territories to the papacy with the exception of Lucca, Florence and Siena.

1125
Florence defeats and absorbs Fiesole.

1186
Work begins on Siena cathedral.

1215
Conflicts between the papacy and Holy Roman Empire (Guelphs and Ghibellines) favour the development of independent city states.

1252
Florence prospers through her textile trade and mints the first gold florin (*fiorino*): merchant guilds achieve wealth and power.

1260
Siena defeats Florence at the Battle of Montaperti.

1302
Dante is exiled from Florence and begins writing *The Divine Comedy*.

1348
The Black Death ravages Tuscany and leads to economic collapse.

1350
The Leaning Tower of Pisa is completed.

1360
Birth of Giovanni di Bicci de' Medici, founder of the Medici banking empire.

1389
Birth of Cosimo de' Medici, greatest member of the Medici dynasty.

1402
Competition held to design Florence's Baptistery doors.

1406
Florence defeats Pisa and gains access to the sea.

1422
Two million florins are in circulation across Europe.

1436
Brunelleschi finishes work on Florence's cathedral dome.

1469
Birth of Machiavelli and the accession of Lorenzo de' Medici, or Lorenzo the Magnificent.

1475
Birth of Michelangelo: Donatello sculpts *David*.

1485
Botticelli paints *The Birth of Venus*.

1494
Florence surrenders to

Cosimo I, Florence's 16th-century Medici ruler

Charles VIII of France: Savonarola, a zealous monk, seizes control of the city.

1498
Savonarola is burned at the stake for heresy and Florence briefly becomes a republic.

1504
Michelangelo sculpts the statue of *David*.

1512
Combined papal and Spanish armies defeat Florence and return the Medici to power.

1537
Cosimo I, a Medici, rules Florence as a Spanish and Austrian puppet.

1570
Cosimo proves his own man and founds the Grand Duchy of Tuscany.

1743
The death of the last Medici sees

Florence and the Grand Duchy pass eventually to Austrian control.

1799
Napoleon defeats Austria and occupies Florence.

1815
Following Napoleon's defeat most of Tuscany is returned by treaty to the Austrians.

1860
The Austrians are defeated and Tuscany joins a united Italy.

1865
Florence is capital of a united Italy until 1871, when Rome is freed from French and papal rule.

1944
Florentine and Tuscan towns and art treasures are damaged by Allied bombing and the retreating Nazis.

1966
After 40 days of rain the Arno bursts its banks and Florence is ravaged by floods.

1993
A terrorist bomb damages part of the Uffizi.

1996
Florence hosts the G7 economic summit.

11

Peace & Quiet

Alpi Apuane

The Apuan Alps contain Tuscany's most spectacular scenery, forming a jagged crest of mountains above the Versilian coast north of Pisa and Lucca. Marble mines streak their western flanks, the source for centuries of stone which has served sculptors from Michelangelo to Henry Moore. On their eastern borders, chestnut-covered slopes fall away to the Garfagnana, a dulcet valley centred on the pleasant little towns of Barga and Caselnuovo (Barga, in particular, is well worth visiting for its lovely cathedral). Well-marked trails criss-cross the slopes, wending through woods or cresting the panoramic and craggy summit ridges. Excellent walking maps of the region are widely available, making it easy to undertake light strolls or proper hikes. Stazzema and Levigliani make good departure points in the west; late May is the best time to see the area's renowned spring flowers. Driving is also a delight, the excellent folk museum in San Pellegrino in Alpe (16km northeast of Castelnuovo) being a particularly good target. The mountains have protected park status, and are earmarked for future national park designation.

Chianti

The rolling hills and vineyards of Chianti make up one of Tuscany's loveliest landscapes

Tuscany's most famous scenic enclave is a region of rambling wooded hills, sunflower-filled fields and vine-covered slopes between Florence and Siena. It is a pretty rather than spectacularly beautiful region, best suited to leisurely exploration by car (▶ 79), bicycle or – given its ever-improving maps – on foot. It is also a surprisingly empty area, its wooded mantle broken only by the occasional farmhouse and small town. Places such as Radda, Gaiole and Castellina are slightly disappointing, often spoilt by new building and a sprawl of light industry, but they are good places to sample Chianti's famous wines. The region is also liberally scattered with remote vineyards, where you can buy directly from local producers: follow one of the many 'wine roads' or look out for the well-signposted *cantine* offering *vendita diretta* (direct sales). Tramping lonely paths or driving gravel roads (*strade bianche*) offer the chance of wildlife sightings: crested porcupines, deer and wild boar, among other creatures, all make the Chianti hills their home.

The spectacular mountains of the Alpi Apuane make excellent walking country

Monte Amiata

Tuscany's fringes are filled with outstanding areas of natural beauty: the Maremma on the coast, for example, or the forests of the Casentino in the east and the meadow topped hills of the Pratomagno, above Arezzo. All these are some way from the region's key towns, however, while Monte Amiata, easily reached from Siena, is one of the area's more convenient scenic retreats. A forested mountain of volcanic origin, its looming profile dominates much of southern Tuscany. Tiny villages cling to its far-flung slopes – Arcidosso, Santa Fiora, Piancastagnaio – all worth a few minutes' attention if you are exploring by car. A road reaches virtually to the summit (1,738m), a popular spot, complete with bars and restaurants, where vast views unfold as far as the sea. Quieter retreats await in the woods below, where you can follow any number of marked trails or find a quiet corner to yourself.

Famous of Tuscany & Florence

Dante, great medieval poet and author of The Divine Comedy

Dante

Dante was born in 1265 into a minor noble family. Educated in Bologna and Padua, he became a civic official and diplomat, eventually joining Florence's ruling Priorate in 1300. He joined a Guelph faction which fell from favour, a change of fortune which led to his forced exile in 1302. Bitterly rejecting his native city, he travelled around Italy, eventually settling in Ravenna. There he probably wrote most of *The Divine Comedy*, an epic poem partly inspired by his doomed love for Beatrice, whom he first met when he was nine and she was eight. He died in 1321 and is buried in Ravenna.

Galileo

Born in Pisa in 1564, the son of a musician, Galileo Galilei moved to Florence in 1574. He was educated in medicine at Pisa, and eventually took up a teaching post in the city, while there he dropped weights from the Leaning Tower to disprove Aristotle's assertion that bodies of different masses fall at different speeds. Later his development of powerful telescopes enabled him to make key discoveries in the field of astronomy. However, his heretical assertion that the earth was not the centre of the heavens led to persecution by the Inquisition. Though saved by his friendship with Pope Urban VII, he remained under house arrest in Florence, where he continued to work until his death in 1642.

Machiavelli

Niccolò Machiavelli was born in Florence in 1469 into an impoverished noble family. 'I learnt to do without', he wrote, 'before I learnt to enjoy'. After entering politics in 1498 he became chancellor and secretary to the war council of the Florentine republic. He spent periods in France, Switzerland and Germany, sojourns which enabled him to view at first hand the machinations of powerful political figures. Following the return of the Medici in 1512 he fell from favour, retiring to write *Il Principe (The Prince)*, a book which brilliantly united political science with the study of human nature. Later he was employed as an advisor to Giuliano de' Medici. He died in 1527.

Girolamo Savonarola
Born in 1452, Savonarola ran away to a Bologna monastery at 23, later moving to San Marco in Florence. By 1491 his apocalyptic sermons were drawing crowds of 10,000 to the Duomo. When Charles VII entered Italy in 1494 causing the Medici to flee, the monk became the city's effective ruler. In 1497 he was excommunicated for criticising Alexander VI, the corrupt Borgia pope, and a year later the Florentines turned against him. He was burned to death in Piazza della Signoria, where a plaque still marks the site of his execution.

Top Ten

1
Campo, Piazza del

Siena's magnificent central piazza and its arc of rosy-coloured palaces make up one of Europe's most beautiful medieval squares.

An arc of palaces and airy open spaces make the Campo one of Europe's loveliest medieval squares

✚ 87C2

✉ Piazza del Campo, Siena

☎ None

🕐 Daily 24 hours

🍴 Many cafés (£–££) and restaurants (£££)

🚍 In the pedestrian zone

♿ Good, but sloping and uneven paving

✋ Free

↔ Duomo (➤ 20), Palazzo Pubblico (➤ 87)

Walking into the Campo from Siena's tight huddle of streets is like stepping on to some medieval stage set. Situated at the heart of the old city, the conch-shaped piazza resembles a vast amphitheatre, its broad sweep of palaces culminating in the battlemented splendour of the Palazzo Pubblico and its attendant bell-tower.

The square probably began life as the Roman forum, becoming the town's principal market-place before taking on its present form in 1293, when the Council of Nine, Siena's governing body, began to buy up land with a view to creating a great central square. The carefully chosen area was at the heart of Siena's *terzi* (the city's three main districts), and was the only piece of land owned by none of Siena's *contrade*, the city's fiercely competitive medieval parishes. As such the Council hoped the square would become the focus of civic life, a physical expression of good government, and a symbol of citizens' loyalty to Siena rather than to factions, families, *terzi* or *contrade*.

The Campo was completed in 1349 with the addition of its brick paving, whose nine sections were designed to symbolise the Council of Nine, and the folds of the Virgin's cloak, sheltering the city under its protective embrace. Both the Palazzo Pubblico and Torre del Mangia are well worth visiting, but you should also indulge in at least one pricey cappuccino at one of the Campo's cafés, an ideal way to take in the square's endless street-life. Be warned, however, most of the restaurants are very expensive.

2
Cappelle Medicee

The Medicis' private chapels and mausoleum feature several of Michelangelo's most outstanding pieces of Florentine funerary sculpture.

The Medici Chapels consist of the Crypt, a mausoleum for minor members of the Medici; the Cappella dei Principi, a vast and opulent chapel dedicated to six of the Medici Grand Dukes; and the Sagrestia Nuova, the last resting place of four of the family's leading lights.

The Crypt is the least interesting area, its sombre, low-ceilinged vaults dotted with the brass-railed tombs of 49 lesser Medici. All were buried pell-mell in 1791 by Ferdinand III, only to be exhumed and re-buried in a more dignified manner in 1857. Steps lead from here to the Cappella dei Principi, begun as a family mausoleum for Cosimo I in 1604. A riot of decoration, this vast, marble-lined chapel was the most expensive project ever commissioned by the Medici. Around the walls, 16 coats of arms represent Medici-controlled Tuscan towns.

A corridor leads to the Sagrestia Nuova (New Sacristy), designed as a contrast to Brunelleschi's Old Sacristy in nearby San Lorenzo. It contains three groups of sculpture (1520–34), two wholly and one partly by Michelangelo. On the left is the tomb of Lorenzo, grandson of Lorenzo the Magnificent, whose statue symbolises the contemplative life. On the right stands the tomb of Giuliano, third son of Lorenzo the Magnificent, symbolising the active life. The third (unfinished) group – a Madonna and Child – was intended as the tomb of Lorenzo the Magnificent and his brother Giuliano.

✚ 28C5

✉ Piazza Madonna degli Aldobrandini, Florence

☎ 055/238 8602

🕐 Daily 8:30am–1:50pm (last admission 30 min before closing). Closed alternate Sun and Mon

🍽 Near by (£)

🚍 In the pedestrian zone: nearest service 1, 6, 7

♿ Few

✋ Expensive

↔ Battistero (▶ 32), Campanile (▶ 33), Duomo (▶ 36–7), San Lorenzo (▶ 54–5), Santa Maria Novella (▶ 58–9)

❓ Visit in conjunction with San Lorenzo (▶ 54–5)

Admiring Michelangelo's sculptures in the Cappelle Medicee

3
Collegiata di
San Gimignano

➕ 64C4

✉ Piazza del Duomo 1, San
Gimignano

☎ 0577/940 316

🕐 Church and Cappella di
Santa Fina: Apr–Sep
daily 9:30-12:30, 3–6;
Oct–Mar daily
9:30–12:30, 3–5:30

🍴 Near by in Piazza della
Cisterna

🚌 In the pedestrian zone

♿ Few: steps up to church

✋ Church: free. Cappella di
Santa Fina: moderate

↔ Museo Civico, Piazza
della Cisterna, Torre
Grossa, Sant'Agostino
(➤ 81–2)

*A series of superbly preserved medieval frescoes
almost completely covers the Collegiata, San
Gimignano's most important church.*

Most people visit the beautiful village of San Gimignano for
its 13 famous medieval towers (➤ 80–2), only to find that
the most memorable part of their visit is the fresco-
covered Collegiata, a church which served as the village's
cathedral until San Gimignano ceased to be a bishopric.
Begun in 1148, but later enlarged, it has little in its simple
Romanesque façade to prepare you for the decorative
splendour inside. Tuscany is filled with fresco cycles, and
those in the Collegiata are not necessarily the region's
most famous, but few cycles are as extensive, and few
have the charm of these lovely paintings. The first panels,
by Taddeo di Bartolo, fill the church's back wall, and depict
the Last Judgement (1393), with Paradise and Hell
portrayed on two adjoining walls. Below is a large St
Sebastian by Benozzo Gozzoli (1420–97), a pupil of Fra
Angelico, well-known for his depictions of contemporary
life and pageantry (➤ 47).

On the church's right-hand (south) wall is a 22-panel
cycle attributed to Lippo Memmi, a 14th century Sienese
artist, which depicts various New Testament scenes from
the Passion and the Life of
Christ. On the opposite wall
are 26 panels (1367) by
Bartolo di Fredi, a cycle of
Old Testament episodes
including scenes from
the stories of Genesis,
Abraham, Joseph, Moses
and Job. To the left of the
high altar, the Cappella di
San Gimignano has a fine
altar (1475) by Benedetto da
Maiano, the sculptor who
was responsible for the
altar, marble shrine and bas-
reliefs in the Cappella di
Santa Fina (top of the right
aisle). This chapel, however,

*San Gimignano's
churches and courtyards
are beautifully decorated
with medieval frescoes*

is better known for its fresco cycle by Domenico
Ghirlandaio (1449–94), another artist whose work reflects
the colour and life of his own period. This cycle depicts
the Life of St Fina, one of San Gimignano's patron saints.
Look out for the fresco which features a 15th-century
view of the town.

4
David

Michelangelo's celebrated statue is one of the most familiar of all Renaissance images, and one of the essential sights of any visit to Florence.

Michelangelo's *David* is exhibited in the Galleria dell'Accademia, Europe's first artistic academy (founded in 1563), together with five other Michelangelo statues and an interesting collection of Gothic and Renaissance paintings. Italy's most famous sculpture was commissioned by the Opera del Duomo in 1501 when Michelangelo was just 26. Its theme – David defeating the tyrant Goliath – was chosen to symbolise the virtues of Florence (then a republic), its freedom from papal and foreign domination, and its recent liberation from Savonarola and the Medici. The marble from which it was sculpted, a vast five-metre block, had been quarried from Carrara some 40 years earlier, but was so thin and riddled with cracks that it had defied the ambitions of all other sculptors. In Michelangelo's hands however, it was transformed in just three years into a work which secured his reputation as the foremost sculptor of his day.

When it was completed 30 leading artists were asked to select a site for the statue. The Piazza della Signoria was their eventual choice. There *David* remained, ravaged by wind and rain, until 1873. The fact that the figure was intended as a piece of outdoor sculpture helps to explain its famous distortions – notably the over-large hands and face – features designed to emphasise its monumentality.

Elsewhere in the gallery are Michelangelo's St *Matthew* (1504–8) and four unfinished *Slaves*, or *Prisoners* (1521–3), the latter a graphic illustration of Michelangelo's dictum that sculpture was the liberation of a form which was already 'imprisoned' in the stone. There are also paintings by such masters as Botticelli, Perugino, Pontormo, Filippino Lippi and others.

✠ 29E5

✉ Via del Ricasoli 60, Florence

☎ 055/238 8609 or 055/238 8612

🕐 Tue–Sat 8:30–6:50, Sun 8:30–1:50. Closed Mon and 1 Jan, 1 May, 25 Dec

🍴 Near by in Piazza San Marco and Via del Ricasoli (£)

🚌 1, 6, 7, 11 and other services to San Marco

♿ Good

✋ Expensive

↔ Museo di San Marco (► 23), Santissima Annunziata (► 53)

❓ Opening times may be subject to variation

Michelangelo's David is one of the supreme works of the Renaissance

5
Duomo di Siena

86B2

Piazza del Duomo, Siena

0577/283 048

Duomo: mid-Mar–Oct, daily 7:30am–7:30pm; Nov–mid-March, daily 7:30–1:30, 2:30–5. Libreria Piccolomini: Jan–mid-Mar, Nov–Dec daily 10–1, 2:30–5; mid-Mar–Oct, daily 9–7:30. Baptistery: Jan–mid-Mar, Nov–Dec, daily 10–1, 2:30–5; mid-Mar–Sep, daily 9–7:30; Oct, daily 9–6

Near by (£)

In the pedestrian zone: occasional shuttle-bus services

None: several steps to main entrance

Duomo: free. Libreria Piccolomini: cheap

Campo (► 16), Museo dell'Opera del Duomo (► 85), Ospedale di Santa Maria della Scala (► 86), Palazzo Pubblico (► 87), Pinacoteca Nazionale (► 88)

A combined ticket is available for entrance to the Libreria Piccolomini, the Baptistery, the Museo dell'Opera del Duomo and the Oratorio di San Bernardino. It is valid for three days and is available at all four locations

The dazzling façade of Siena's cathedral is a masterpiece of Romanesque and Gothic architecture

This magnificent Gothic cathedral boasts one of Italy's loveliest façades and an interior bursting with a variety of outstanding works of art.

Siena's cathedral was begun in 1196 and completed in 1376, during which time there was an aborted attempt to extend the building, a scheme whose half-finished results can be seen in the skeletal shell to the right of the present structure. Much of the lower part of the façade (1285) was designed by Giovanni Pisano, though most of his original statuary is now in the nearby Museo dell'Opera.

The exterior's distinctive black-and-white banding is echoed in the interior's monochrome pavement, which consists of 56 panels (1349–1547) created over the centuries by some of Siena's leading artists. Mid-way down the left aisle (fourth altar) stands the Piccolomini altar, whose four lower-niche statues are early works by Michelangelo. Alongside lies the entrance to the Libreria Piccolomini, beautifully frescoed by Pinturicchio with scenes from the life of Aeneas Piccolomini (1509), a Tuscan nobleman who became Pope Pius II.

At the end of the left aisle stands the Duomo's masterpiece: Nicola Pisano's Gothic pulpit (1268). To its left, in the corner chapel, is Tino da Camaino's influential Tomb of Cardinal Petroni (1318). Below it lies Donatello's bronze pavement Tomb of Bishop Pecci (1426). The circular Cappella di San Giovanni in the left transept has a bronze statue of John the Baptist by Donatello and more Pinturicchio frescoes. A similar chapel in the opposite transept, the Cappella Chigi, was designed by Bernini. To the rear of the cathedral be sure to visit the Baptistery, which features swathes of lovely 15th-century frescoes and a font with bronze panels by Ghiberti, Donatello and Jacopo della Quercia.

6
Museo Nazionale del Bargello

✚ 29E3

✉ Via del Proconsolo 4, Florence

Italy's greatest collection of Renaissance sculpture is contained in the Bargello, together with an array of majolica, tapestries, paintings and silverware.

The fortress-like Bargello, begun in 1255, was Florence's earliest civic palace, serving first as the city's seat of government and later as the home of the chief of police. Later still it became a prison, torture chamber and place of execution, assuming its present role in 1865. The museum spreads over three floors, though its key works are found in just two large rooms. The first lies to the right of the ticket hall, and concentrates on the late Renaissance works of Michelangelo, Giambologna and Benvenuto Cellini. Michelangelo is represented by three contrasting works: a delicate *tondo* of the Madonna and Child, a powerful portrait bust of Brutus, and a lurching, soft-bellied statue of Bacchus. Other highlights include a bronze of Cosimo I by Cellini and Giambologna's celebrated Mercury, a sublime study in speed.

From this first room, wander into the courtyard, glance at the exterior sculptures in the small rooms opposite, and then climb the external staircase to the first floor. At the top of the stairs is a wonderful menagerie of bronze animals by Giambologna. Turn right and you come to the museum's second major room, a glorious vaulted hall filled with sculptural masterpieces. Look out in particular for the works of Donatello, notably his St George, removed from Orsanmichele, the Marzocco, Florence's heraldic lion, and the debonair and famously androgynous statue of David. Subsequent rooms are crammed with all manner of interesting rugs, tapestries, glassware, silverware and many other precious objets d'art. Particularly noteworthy is the Salone del Camino, which contains Italy's most important collection of small bronzes.

☎ 055/238 8606

🕐 Daily 8:30–1:50. Closed alternate Sun and Mon, and 1 Jan, 25 Apr, 1 May, 25 Dec

🍴 Near by in Via del Proconsolo (£)

🚌 19

♿ Good: lift to upper floor

💵 Moderate

↔ Museo di Firenze com'era (➤ 40), Palazzo Vecchio (➤ 50), Piazza della Signoria (➤ 51)

A delicate marble frieze by Francesco Rustici, one of many masterpieces in the Bargello

7
Museo di San Marco

The ancient Dominican convent of San Marco is renowned for a series of sublime frescoes and paintings by Fra Angelico.

San Marco was originally owned by Vallombrosan and Sylvestrine monks, passing to the Dominicans in 1436, when it was restored at Cosimo de' Medici's personal expense. Its subsequent priors included Fra Angelico, not only a devout Dominican, but also one of the finest of Florence's early Renaissance painters. Today the convent buildings are a museum given over almost entirely to the artist's paintings and frescoes.

Many of the paintings are contained in the Ospizio dei Pellegrini, a room once used to provide pilgrims with food and shelter (located off the main cloister). Its two masterpieces hang on opposite walls: a Deposition (1440), removed from the church of Santa Trínita, and the Madonna dei Linaiuoli (1433), commissioned for the headquarters of the flax-makers' (*linaiuoli*) guild. Also off the cloister is the Sala Capitolare, or Chapter House, which features a Crucifixion (1442) by Fra Angelico. The Refectory near by contains a large fresco of the Last Supper by Domenico Ghirlandaio (beyond the shop).

Steps from the cloister lead to the first floor, where you are greeted by Fra Angelico's famous

✚ 29E6

✉ Piazza San Marco, Florence

☎ 055/238 8608

🕐 Daily 8:30–2. Closed alternate Sun and Mon, and 1 Jan, 1 May, 15 Aug, 25 Dec

🍴 Near by in Piazza San Marco (£)

🚌 1, 6, 7, 10, 11, 17, 20, 25, 31, 32, 33

♿ Good

✋ Expensive

↔ *David*, Galleria dell'Accademia (➤ 19), Palazzo Medici-Riccardi (➤ 47)

Annunciation (c.1445), one of the most beautiful of all Renaissance paintings. The rest of the floor is largely taken up by 44 dormitory cells, each frescoed by Fra Angelico and his pupils with religious scenes intended as aids to monastic devotion. At the end of the far corridor are three cells once occupied by Savonarola. At the end of the corridor on your right are two cells, larger than the rest, once used by Cosimo il Vecchio de' Medici. Close by is Europe's first public library, designed for Cosimo by Michelozzo in 1441.

The San Marco museum contains numerous paintings by Fra Angelico and other Renaissance artists

8
Santa Croce

✝ 29F2

✉ Piazza Santa Croce, Florence

☎ 055/244 619 or 234 2289

🕐 Santa Croce: daily 8–12:30, 3–6:30. Museo dell'Opera di Santa Croce and Cappella dei Pazzi: Mar–Sep, Thu–Tue 10–12:30, 2:30–6:30; Oct–Feb, Thu–Tue 10–12:30, 3–5. Closed Wed

🍴 Near by in Piazza Santa Croce (£)

🚌 13, 23, shuttle bus B

♿ Good

✋ Santa Croce: free. Museo dell'Opera di Santa Croce and Cappella dei Pazzi: cheap

↔ Museo Nazionale del Bargello (► 22), Museo Bardini (► 40)

The most famous church in Florence is celebrated for its superb Giotto frescoes and the tombs of Galileo, Michelangelo and Machiavelli.

Begun in 1294 by Arnolfo di Cambio, and completed in 1450, this Franciscan foundation attracted the attention of many wealthy families, all anxious to seek spiritual salvation by being buried among the 'humble' Franciscans; hence the many tombs and the various frescoed family chapels (notably those of the Bardi, Peruzzi and Baroncelli).

Among those buried in the church are Michelangelo (first tomb on the right), Machiavelli (sixth on the right) and Galileo (first on the left). There are also outstanding examples of Renaissance funerary sculpture, notably 15th-century works by Bernardo Rossellino (end of the right aisle) and Desiderio da Settignano (end of the left aisle). More famous still are the church's fresco cycles, the best known of which are by Giotto, who was responsible for the paintings in the Cappella Bardi and the Cappella Peruzzi (adjacent chapels to the right of the high altar).

To the right of the church lie the Cappella dei Pazzi (1430) and the Museo dell'Opera di Santa Croce. The former, rather austere chapel by Brunelleschi, is simply decorated with 12 terracotta *tondi* of the Apostles by Luca della Robbia, who also decorated the portico, and polychrome roundels in the upper corners (attributed to Brunelleschi and Donatello). The Museo's highlights are Donatello's St Louise of Toulouse and a Crucifix by Cimabue.

9
Torre Pendente
(Leaning Tower)

Few sights are as immediately recognisable as the Leaning Tower of Pisa, one of several monuments in Pisa's beautiful Campo dei Miracoli.

Pisa's famous Leaning Tower was begun in 1173 as a companion piece for the city's Duomo and Baptistery, two buildings which make up a lovely medieval ensemble in a green-lawned square known as the Campo dei Miracoli (the 'Field of Miracles'). The tower began to lean almost from the outset, tilting into the sandy subsoil under the foundations (this part of the coast was once under water, so that local soil is composed almost entirely of sand and silt). Initial construction work on the tower was abandoned after only three storeys were complete, but work resumed in the 13th century when it was accepted that the tower would not fall. Over the next 180 years a series of architects tried to correct the lean by adding off-centre sections. None were successful. Today the tower is a dizzying 5.2m to the vertical.

Architects and engineers have long agonised over how to prevent the tower's collapse. One plan is to drill out soil from one side to encourage the tower to lean back towards the upright. Another suggests burying ten 100-tonne anchors attached to a concrete ring (already being built) to 'pull' or hold the tower steady. Yet another recommends applying 'electro-osmosis' to one side of the tower, a system whereby electrodes 20m below the surface would draw moisture from the sub-soil. This would cause the soil to dry and contract, leading to a gradual settling of the tower. So far the most successful measure has been to strap an unsightly several hundred tonnes of lead to the tower's northern side, a step which over a nine-month period halted the tower's movement and pulled it back 2.5cm towards the vertical.

64B5

Campo (Piazza) dei Miracoli, Pisa

050/560 921

Interior closed to the public until further notice

Near by (£)

Bus (no 1) from railway station

Campo dei Miracoli: good

Campo dei Miracoli: free

Duomo, Baptistery and Camposanto (► 77)

The Leaning Tower began to tilt almost from the moment it was built in 1173

10
Uffizi, Galleria degli

✝ 29D2

✉ Loggiato degli Uffizi, off Piazza della Signoria, Florence

☎ 055/23 885 or 238 8651

🕐 Tue–Sat 9–7, Sun 9–2. Last admission 45 min before closing. Closed Mon and 1 Jan, Easter Sun, 1 May, 15 Aug, 25 Dec

🍴 Café (£)

🚌 In the pedestrian zone

♿ Good

✋ Expensive

↔ Museo di Storia della Scienza (► 45), Orsanmichele (► 46), Palazzo Vecchio (► 50), Piazza della Signoria (► 51), Ponte Vecchio (► 52)

❓ Queues for the Uffizi can be long: a system may be introduced of pre-booked tickets for admittance at set times. Consult tourist office for latest details

One of the world's finest art galleries, the Uffizi contains a collection of paintings which features all the great names of the Florentine Renaissance.

The building housing the Uffizi was begun by Vasari in 1560, its original purpose being to serve as a suite of offices (*uffizi*) from which the Medici could administer the Grand Duchy of Tuscany. In 1737 it was bequeathed to Florence, along with the Medici art collection, by Anna Luisa, sister of Gian Gastone, the last Medici Grand Duke. Today its 45 rooms house not only the cream of 14th- and

15th-century Florentine paintings, but also masterpieces from elsewhere in Italy (notably Venice and Siena), together with a surprising number of major works from Germany, Holland and Spain. Rooms 1–15 are given over to the Florentine Renaissance (and contain the most famous paintings); rooms 16–27 concentrate on the age of High Renaissance and Mannerism, and rooms 28–45 are devoted to later Italian and European paintings.

Highlights are too numerous to mention, though certain works deserve extra special attention. Room 2 opens with altarpieces of the *Maestà* (*Madonna Enthroned*) by Giotto, Duccio and Cimabue, three of Italy's greatest 13th-century painters, who contributed to the movement towards naturalism and emotion and away from the stilted and more styliszed Byzantine approach to subjects in art. Room 3's Sienese paintings are dominated by Simone Martini's sublime *Annunciation*, while in rooms 5 and 6 the key work is Gentile da Fabriano's exquisitely detailed *Adoration of the Magi*. Rooms 10–14 feature paintings by Botticelli, notably the famous *Primavera* and *Birth of Venus*. Room 18 is best known for the *Venus de' Medici*, renowned for centuries as one of antiquity's most erotic statues. Successive rooms feature works by, among others, Raphael, Caravaggio and Michelangelo; the Venetians Titian, Giorgione and Carpaccio; and Europeans such as Rembrandt, Rubens and Van Dyck.

A Madonna by Filippo Lippi, one of the Uffizi's countless masterpieces

26

What To See

CENTRAL FLORENCE (FIRENZE)

Palazzo dei Congressi
PIAZZA DELLA INDIPENDENZA
VIA VAL FONDA
VIA FAENZA
VIA GUELFA
VIA JACOPO DA DIACETTO
VIA LUIGI ALAMANNI
PIAZZA ADUA
autobus
VIA NAZIONALE
Mercato Centrale
PIAZZA DEL MERCATO CENTRALE
VIA DEGLI ORTI ORICELLARI
Stazione Centrale di Santa Maria Novella
PIAZZA DELLA STAZIONE
VIA FAENZA
Cappelle Medicee
San Lorenzo
VIA SANTA CATERINA
PIAZZA DELL' UNITÀ ITALIANA
PIAZZA DI MADONNA DEGLI ALDOBRANDINI
VIA PALAZZUOLO
VIA DELLA SCALA
Santa Maria Novella
VIA DE' PANZANI
Biblioteca Laurenziana
PIAZZA SANTA MARIA NOVELLA
VIA DEI BANCHI
VIA DE' CERRETANI
Battistero
VIA DEI PECORI
Ognissanti
BORGO OGNISSANTI
PIAZZA OGNISSANTI
VIA DELLE BELLE DONNE
VIA DELLE
San Pancrazio
VIA DELLA SPADA
VIA DE' VECCHIETTI
VIA ROMA
LUNGARNO AMERIGO VESPUCCI
Arno
Palazzo Rucellai
VIA DELLA VIGNA NUOVA
VIA DE' TORNABUONI
VIA DEGLI STROZZI
PIAZZA DELLA REPUBBLICA
PIAZZA C. GOLDONI
Palazzo Corsini
Santa Trinita
Palazzo Strozzi
VIA DEI SASSETTI
Poste
CALIMALA
LUNGARNO SODERINI
PIAZZA D'CESTELIO
PONTE ALLA CARRAIA
LUNGARNO CORSINI
PIAZZA SANTA TRINITA
VIA PORTA ROSSA
Palazzo Davanzati
VIA POR
Palazzo di Parte Guelfa
SANTA MARIA
BORGO SAN FREDIANO
LUNGARNO GUICCIARDINI
VIA DI SANTO SPIRITO
PONTE SANTA TRINITA
LUNGARNO ACCIAIUOLI
Santi Apostoli
Santo Stefano
LUNGARNO ARCHIBUSIERI
PIAZZA DEL CARMINE
VIA SANTA MONACA
BORGO SAN JACOPO
Ponte Vecchio
Santa Maria del Carmine / Cappella Brancacci
VIA SANT'AGOSTINO
Santo Spirito
VIA MAGGIO
PIAZZA SANTA FELICITA
VIA DELLA CHIESA
VIA DEI SERRAGLI
PIAZZA SANTO SPIRITO
VIA MAZZETTA
VIA DE' GUICCIARDINI
Santa Felicita
Palazzo Guicciardini
Casa Guidi
PIAZZA DEI PITTI
VIA ROMANA
Palazzo Pitti
Giardino di Boboli
Palazzina della Meridiana

0   100   200   300 m

A   B   C

1 2 3 4 5 6

Florence

Florence is a city-sized shrine to the Renaissance, its streets filled with churches and monuments, its galleries overflowing with some of Europe's greatest paintings and sculptures. Five centuries ago the city was almost without equal, its artistic and intellectual ferment unparalleled, its wealth virtually unsurpassed. Patronage from families such as the Medici provided the spur for innovation, creating an atmosphere in which creativity and individual genius flourished as never before.

Yet Florence today is far more than a vast museum. The Giardino di Boboli provides welcome green space; bustling street markets offer life and colour; and tiny back alleys hide intimate medieval nooks and artisans' workshops. Tree-lined squares harbour sun-drenched cafés, while restaurants and ice-cream parlours abound, as alluring as any painting or sculpture.

'...Beautiful
The city lies along the
ample vale,
Cathedral, tower and
palace, piazza and street,
The river trailing like a
silver cord...'

ELIZABETH BARRETT BROWNING
(1806–61), *Aurora Leigh*

Florence

Florence is compact and easily explored on foot, though its wealth of art and culture, and the way sights are scattered across the city, means it is difficult to plan convenient sightseeing itineraries. The historic centre conforms to the grid of the old Roman colony, its principal points of interest lying on and around two main squares: Piazza del Duomo and Piazza della Signoria.

Most people begin a tour of the city in Piazza del Duomo, where you should see the Duomo (cathedral), Baptistery and Museo dell'Opera, as well as climbing the Campanile or cathedral dome for a superb view of the city. Close by lies the Museo Nazionale del Bargello, Italy's greatest collection of Renaissance sculpture. Via dei Calzaiuoli, Florence's pedestrianised main street, leads south to Piazza della Signoria, where you should visit the Palazzo Vecchio, the Uffizi – Italy's most famous art gallery – and the nearby Museo di Storia della Scienza.

North of the central district the key sights are the Cappelle Medicee, with statues by Michelangelo, the Accademia (home to Michelangelo's *David*) and the Palazzo Medici-Riccardi, with its lovely fresco cycle. A little further north lies the Museo di San Marco, filled with sublime paintings by Fra Angelico. The city's two most important churches – Santa Croce and Santa Maria Novella – lie east and west of the centre respectively. Across the Arno, the river which divides the city, is a quieter district known as the Oltrarno, worth visiting for the Cappella Brancacci and its fresco cycle, and the Palazzo Pitti, home to a superb collection of Medici art and artefacts.

'I have seldom seen a city,' *wrote Percy Bysshe Shelley*, 'so lovely at first sight as Florence'

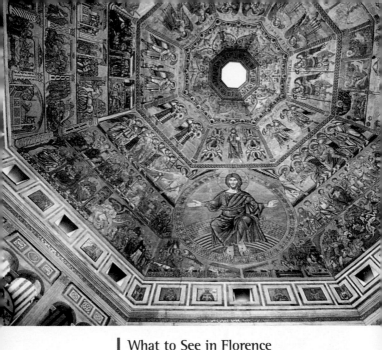

What to See in Florence

🕂 29D4
✉ Piazza San Giovanni,
Piazza del Duomo
☎ 055/230 2885 or 294 514
🕓 Mon–Sat 1:30–6:30, Sun
and religious hols
8:30–1:30. Closed 1 Jan,
Easter Sun, 24 Jun, 25–6
Dec
🍴 Near by (£)
🚌 1, 6, 7, 11, 14, 23
♿ Good
💷 Cheap
🔄 Campanile (▶ 33),
Duomo (▶ 36–7), Museo
dell'Opera del Duomo
(▶ 44)

BATTISTERO ✪✪✪

The Baptistery of Florence was long believed to have been a Roman temple to Mars; the disovery of pavement fragments has confirmed the existence of a 1st-century palace on the site, though the core of the present building probably dates from the 6th–7th centuries. The marble decoration of the classically inspired exterior, remodelled in the 11th century, was to inspire generations of architects and provide the model for countless Tuscan churches.

The south doors (1328–36), the work of Andrea Pisano, depict scenes from the life of St John the Baptist (the patron saint of Florence), and were cast by Venetian bell-makers, then Europe's most accomplished bronze smiths. A famous competition was arranged in 1401 to award the commission for the north doors (1403–24), an event widely considered to have marked the 'beginning' of the Renaissance. It was won by Lorenzo Ghiberti, also responsible for the east doors (1425–52), works so exquisite they are often known as the 'Gates of Paradise' (the original panels are now in the Museo dell'Opera, ▶ 44).

Inside, the highlights are the mosaic ceiling (begun in 1225), created by Venetian mosaicists, and the glorious tessellated marble pavement, at whose heart you can still see the outlines of the building's original font (all Florentine children were once baptised here). Less eye-catching are the fine mosaic frieze; the lovely upper gallery, and – to the right of the apse, or *scarsella* – the distinctive *Tomb of the Antipope John XXIII* (1427) by Donatello and Michelozzo.

The Baptistery's 13th-century mosaic ceiling is largely the work of Venetian craftsmen

CAMPANILE ✪✪

The multi-hued Campanile is one of Italy's most beautiful bell-towers, and the views from its pinnacle are a highlight of any visit to Florence. At 85m, it is just 6m lower than the Duomo, its near neighbour, and to reach the summit you have to climb 414 steps (there is no lift).

Begun in 1334, the tower was probably designed by Giotto, who laboured on the project during his reign as city architect and *capo maestro* (head of works). At his death in 1337, however, only the base – the first of the tower's present five levels – was complete. Work on the second storey (1337–42) was supervised by Andrea Pisano, fresh from his labours on the Baptistery's north doors. When he moved on, responsibility passed to Francesco Talenti, who completed the decoration and the remaining three storeys (1348–59).

Most of the Campanile's many reliefs – probably designed by Giotto – are copies, the originals now residing in the Museo dell'Opera. Two sets decorate the first storey, the lower tier in hexagonal frames, the upper tier in diamonds. The hexagonal reliefs, by Pisano and his pupils, depict the Creation, the Arts and Industries and the Seven Sacraments. The Five Liberal Arts (Grammar, Philosophy, Music, Arithmetic and Astronomy) on the northern face are by Luca della Robbia. The upper reliefs, also the work of Pisano, portray the Seven Planets and Seven Virtues. On the second storey, the niche sculptures of the Sibyls and Prophets are copies of works by Donatello and others, now in the Museo dell'Opera.

✚ 29D4
✉ Piazza del Duomo
☎ 055/230 2885, 294 514 or 271 071
🕐 Daily 9–4:50. Closing times indicate last admission: tower remains open 50 min thereafter. Closed 1 Jan, Easter Sun, 8 Sep, 25–6 Dec
🍴 Near by (£)
🚌 1, 6, 7, 11, 14, 23
♿ None
💵 Moderate
↔ Battistero (► 32), Duomo (► 36–7), Museo dell'Opera del Duomo (► 44)

Climb to the top of Florence's famous bell-tower for some superb views of the city

28A2

Santa Maria del Carmine, Piazza del Carmine

055/238 2195

Mon, Wed–Sat 10–5, Sun and public hols 1–5. Closed Tue, Easter Sun, 25 Dec

Near by (£)

Shuttle bus B

Few

Moderate

Giardino di Boboli (➤ 38), Palazzo Pitti (➤ 48–9), Ponte Vecchio (➤ 52)

Entered via the cloisters of Santa Maria del Carmine (to the right of the church façade)

CAPPELLA BRANCACCI ✪✪✪

On its own, the church of Santa Maria del Carmine would merit little attention. Constructed between 1268 and 1422, it was almost completely rebuilt after a disastrous fire in 1771. One of the areas that survived the conflagration, however, was the Cappella Brancacci, a tiny chapel decorated with one of the most important and influential fresco cycles in Western art. It was commissioned in 1424 by Felice Brancacci, a former Florentine ambassador to Egypt, and its decoration entrusted to Masolino da Panicale (1383–1447) and his young assistant, Tommaso di Ser Giovanni di Mone Cassai (better known by his nickname Masaccio, or 'Mad Tom'). In 1426 Masaccio's burgeoning talents were given fuller rein when Masolino was recalled to Budapest, where he was employed as a painter to the Hungarian court.

In his absence Masaccio demonstrated a mastery of perspective, narrative drama and bold naturalism not seen in Florence since the days of Giotto. Masolino returned in 1427, but was called away to Rome a year later. Masaccio followed him after a few months, and neither painter worked in the chapel again. Masaccio died in the Holy City in 1428, aged just 28. In 1436 Brancacci was exiled by Cosimo de' Medici, leaving the frescoes untouched until their completion by Filippino Lippi in 1485. All but two of the frescoes depict scenes from the Life of St Peter, and all of them are outstanding, but note in particular Masaccio's very powerful panel of *Adam and Eve Banished from Paradise* (top tier, extreme left). It is an excellent illustration of Masaccio's clever employment of stark and angular figures to portray profound emotion.

The Cappella Brancacci and its pioneering Renaissance fresco cycle

CASA BUONARROTI ✪

The Casa Buonarroti, bought by Michelangelo in 1508, is often described as the sculptor's house (Michelangelo's surname was Buonarroti). In fact the maestro never lived here; the present house, its decoration and its collection of Michelangelo memorabilia were arranged by his nephew Leonardo (his sole descendant), and subsequently by Leonardo's son, Michelangelo the Younger. The house, if a little impersonal, is beautifully presented, its smart appearance the result of expensive restoration following the 1966 flood. The admission charge is a touch overpriced, however, especially given the fact that the museum contains only four minor works and a handful of drawings by the master. At the same time, the maze of decorated rooms, antique furniture, frescoed ceilings and various *objets d'art* are all attractive in their own right.

➕ 29F3
✉ Via Ghibellina 70
☎ 055/241 752
🕐 Mon, Wed–Sun
9:30–1:30. Closed Tue
and 1 Jan, Easter Sun,
25 April, 1 May, 15 Aug,
25–6 Dec
🍴 Near by (£)
🚌 13, 19, 23, shuttle bus B
♿ Good
💰 Expensive
↔ Santa Croce (▶ 24)

The Battle of the Centaurs, *a marble relief by Michelangelo in the Casa Buonarroti*

The sculptural highlights are on the first floor. The earliest, the *Madonna della Scala* (1491), is a delicate, shallow relief showing the influence of Donatello. Carved when Michelangelo was still in his teens, it is 'the masters' earliest known work. Near by stands the *Battle of the Centaurs* (1492), a more complex work executed when Michelangelo was employed by Lorenzo the Magnificent. The adjoining room features a wooden model of Michelangelo's plan for the façade of San Lorenzo (never realised), together with a sprawling wood-and-wax model of a torso, part of a huge river god, possibly intended for the Cappelle Medicee. A room to the right contains a slender Crucifix, a work believed lost until its discovery in 1965.

29D4
Piazza del Duomo
055/230 2885, 271 071
or 294 514

DUOMO (SANTA MARIA DEL FIORE)

The first church on the site of Santa Maria del Fiore, Florence's magnificent cathedral, was built in the 7th century and dedicated to Santa Reparata, an obscure Syrian or Palestinian saint and martyr (San Lorenzo and the Baptistery served as Florence's cathedral for much of the city's early history). In the 13th century, when Florence was a prosperous and sophisticated metropolis, the city's elders declared the old church too 'crudely built and too small for such a city'. They envisaged something to rival the new cathedrals of Siena and Pisa – something, as an edict of 1294 put it, of the 'most exalted and most prodigal magnificence, in order that the industry and power of men may never create or undertake anything whatsoever more vast and more beautiful'.

Responsibility for designing this magnificence was entrusted to Arnolfo di Cambio in 1294. After his death, six years later, work lapsed until 1331, Giotto taking over as the building's master of works in 1334. Construction of the vast Gothic nave, the tribunes (apses) and the drum of the colossal dome was finally completed in 1418.

The cathedral's interior is strikingly austere. It is also breathtaking in size – it can accommodate some 10,000 people – and ranks as Europe's fourth largest church after St Peter's and the cathedrals of Milan and St Paul's in London. The highlights include two large frescoed equestrian portraits on the north (left) wall: one of the English mercenary Sir John Hawkwood (1436) by Paolo Uccello, the other of Niccolò da Tolentino (1456) – another soldier of fortune – by Andrea del Castagno. Note, too, the clock above the main door by Paolo Uccello and the *Tomb of Antonio d'Orso* (1323) to its right, the work of Mino da Fiesole. Much of the stained glass in the apses was designed by Lorenzo Ghiberti, as was the superb reliquary (1432–42) in the middle (third) chapel of the central apse.

The cathedral's main highlight, however, is its vast dome, one of the supreme feats of late medieval engineering. Designed by Brunelleschi, who won the commission in 1418, it was built using many innovative techniques which are still shrouded in mystery. The key to the project's success was the construction of an inner and an outer shell, as well as the use of a herringbone pattern of bricks arranged in cantilevered rings (allowing the dome to support itself as it rose). Its interior is decorated with frescoes of the *Last Judgement* (1572–9) by Vasari, much criticised over the centuries as unworthy of so great a building. They pale into insignificance alongside the view from the dome's lantern, which is reached by steps from the top of the north (left) aisle.

GALLERIA DELL' ACCADEMIA (▶ 19, TOP TEN)

⏱ Cathedral: summer Mon–Sat 9–6, winter Mon–Sat 10–5, except first Sat of the month 10–3:30, Sun 1–5. Closed on public hols. Dome: Mon–Fri 8:30–6:20, first Sat of the month 10–3:20, otherwise Sat 8:30–5. Crypt (Santa Reparata): Mon–Sat 10–5

🍴 Near by (£)

🚌 1, 6, 7, 11, 14, 23

♿ Good

💷 Cathedral: free. Dome: moderate. Crypt: cheap

↔ Campanile (▶ 33), Battistero (▶ 32), Museo dell'Opera del Duomo (▶ 44)

Did you know ?

The Duomo's façade and its striking Tuscan marbles – green from Prato, white from Carrara and red from the Maremma – is surprisingly recent. Arnolfo di Cambio's original façade, which was only a quarter finished, was pulled down in 1587, and replaced at the end of the 19th century following a competition in which some 92 designs were submitted.

Florence's beautiful marble-clad cathedral and its famous dome, one of the miracles of medieval engineering

GIARDINO DI BOBOLI

Italy's favourite gardens were begun in 1549, when the
Medici moved to the nearby Palazzo Pitti. They were
opened to the public in 1766. Today they are one of the
loveliest places in the city to rest, picnic or take a siesta.
They also offer sweeping views of the Florentine skyline,
notably from the belvederes beside the rococo *Kaffeehaus*
and the unkempt Giardino del Cavaliere. From the Palazzo
Pitti's main courtyard, where the gardens are entered,
paths lead to the Amphitheatre, a large arena designed to
house Medici entertainments (it was built over the quarry
used for the Palazzo's building stone). Sightseeing
highlights include many antique, Renaissance and
Mannerist statues; countless fountains (especially
Ganymede and *Neptune*); and the Viottolone, a long,
statue-lined avenue of cypresses which culminates in the
Isolotto, a pretty, moated island garden. The gardens also
contain the small Museo della Porcellana, a collection of
antique porcelain, which can be visited on a combined
ticket with the Galleria del Costume and Museo degli
Argenti (➤ 48–9). Free maps of the garden (in Italian text)
are sometimes available on request at the ticket office.

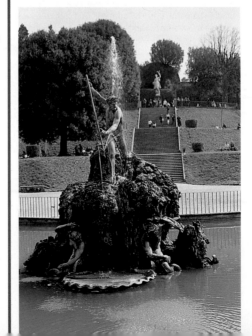

*The Fontana del Nettuno
is one of many striking
fountains in the Boboli
Gardens; opposite, the
medieval kitchen of the
Antica Casa Fiorentina*

MUSEO DELLA ANTICA CASA FIORENTINA ★★

This beautiful medieval house offers a wonderful insight into how Florence's artists, merchants and noble families might once have lived, as well as providing a vivid context for paintings and sculptures which can sometimes seem rather lifelessly displayed in the city's museums and galleries. The house was built in about 1330 for the Davizzi, a family of wealthy wool merchants. It was then sold to the Davanzati, who remained the owners until 1838. It opened as a museum in 1910 and was bought by the state in 1951.

In the entrance courtyard, which immediately sets the medieval tone, store rooms to the rear were kept stocked in case of siege or famine, while a private well served the house with water, a luxury in an age when most water was still drawn from public fountains. The age-old wooden staircase, the only one of its kind in Florence, leads to the first of the three floors, each of which is dotted with beautifully furnished rooms and evocative medieval corners.

Highlights of the first floor include the Sala dei Pappagalli, named after the parrots (pappagalli) adorning its frescoes, and the gorgeous Sala Pavoni or Camera Nuziale (Wedding Room). The latter features a glorious 14th-century Sicilian bedspread, a two-winged tabernacle by Neri di Bicci and a lovely frescoed frieze of trees, peacocks (pavoni) and exotic birds. The third floor is given over to the delightful palace kitchen, a room often situated on the upper floor of medieval houses to minimise damage in the event of fire.

⊕ 28C3

✉ Palazzo Davanzati, Via Porta Rossa 13

☎ 055/238 8610

◷ Usually Tue–Sat 9–2, first and third Sun of the month 9–2 (see note below). Last admission 30 min before closing. Closed Mon, second and fourth Sun of the month and 1 Jan, 1 May, 25–6 Dec

🍴 Near by in Piazza della Repubblica (£)

🚌 In the pedestrian zone: nearest services 6, 11, 31, 32, 37 to Piazza Santa Trínita

♿ Good

✋ Moderate

↔ Orsanmichele (►46), Palazzo Vecchio (►50), Piazza della Signoria (►51), Ponte Vecchio (►52), Santa Trínita (►63),

❓ The museum closed in 1995 for long-term restoration: consult tourist office for latest details

+ 29E1
⊠ Piazza de' Mozzi
☎ 055/234 2427
🕐 Mon, Tue, Thu–Sat 9–2,
  Sun 8–1. Last admission
  1 hour before closing.
  Closed Wed and 1 Jan,
  Easter Sun, 1 May, 15
  Aug, 25–6 Dec
🍴 Near by on Lungarno
  Serristori (£)
🚌 Shuttle buses B and C
♿ Good
👣 Moderate
↔ Giardino di Boboli (►
  38), Palazzo Pitti
  (► 48–9)

MUSEO BARDINI

Unjustifiably ignored by most visitors, the Museo Bardini was created by Stefano Bardini, a 19th-century art dealer whose own collection became too large for his home, and was transferred to this ersatz 'palace' created from doors, ceilings and fireplaces salvaged from demolished medieval buildings.

The exhibits are housed in some 20 rooms ranged over two floors. On the ground floor rooms 7 and 8 feature some of the museum's highlights, notably a Cosmati pulpit, a tiny carved head attributed to Nicola Pisano, and a stunning Gothic *aedicule* (canopy) framing a statue of Charity by Tino da Camaino.

The first floor begins with armour and medieval weaponry, before proceeding to Room 14, which features two of the collection's treasures: a terracotta *Madonna and Child* and the collage-like *Madonna dei Cordai*, both attributed to Donatello. Successive rooms offer a bewitching miscellany of reliefs, furniture and majolica. Room 20 boasts two magnificently inland choir stalls and one of the city's grandest wooden ceilings.

+ 29E4
⊠ Via dell'Oriuolo 24
☎ 055/239 8483
🕐 Mon–Wed, Fri, Sat 9–2,
  Sun 8–1. Closed Thu and
  1 Jan, Easter Sun, 1 May,
  15 Aug, 25–6 Dec
🍴 Near by (£)
🚌 14, 23, shuttle bus B
♿ Few: garden approach
  and some steps
👣 Cheap
↔ Museo Nazionale del
  Bargello (► 22), Duomo
  (► 36–7), Museo
  dell'Opera del Duomo
  (► 44)

MUSEO DI FIRENZE COM' ERA

This is one of the city's most interesting minor museums, thanks to a collection of paintings, engraving and topographical drawings evoking the Florence of days gone by. The first room contains its principal treasure, the *Pianta della Catena*, a vast panorama of the city as it appeared in 1470. The room to its right features lunette paintings (1599) of the Medici villas by the Flemish painter van Utens – among the loveliest things in any Florentine museum.

Other highlights include the engravings of Telemaco Signorini (1874), and a vaulted room devoted to drawings and engravings of the city's major buildings.

A lunette of a Medici villa in The Museo di Firenze com'era

A Walk from the Ponte Vecchio to San Miniato al Monte

This mainly uphill walk takes in some of the key sights of the Oltrarno, and can easily be extended to embrace another three: the Palazzo Pitti (▶48–9), Giardino di Boboli (▶38) and Cappella Brancacci (▶34). As a less strenuous option, it can also be walked in reverse, downhill, by catching a 12 or 13 bus to Piazzale Michelangelo or San Miniato al Monte.

Cross the Ponte Vecchio and follow Via de' Guicciardini to Piazza Santa Felicita.

Santa Felicita, probably Florence's second oldest church after San Lorenzo, is noted for Brunelleschi's *Cappella Capponi*, celebrated in turn for Pontormo's *Deposition* (1525–8), a masterpiece of Mannerist painting.

Take the lane left of the church and turn immediately left to Via de' Bardi. Turn right and follow Via de' Bardi. Continue to Piazza de' Mozzi if you wish to visit the Museo Bardini. Otherwise turn right and dog-leg up Costa Scarpuccia. Turn left on Costa di San Giorgio.

Number 19 Costa di San Giorgio was the home of Galileo. At the top of the street lies Porta San Giorgio (1258), the city's oldest surviving gateway. To the right is the entrance to the Forte di Belvedere (1590–95), built by Buontalenti for Ferdinand I. The views of the city from its ramparts are wonderful.

At Porta San Giorgio turn right and follow Via di Belvedere and the city walls for marvellous views over olive groves and the distant hills. At Porta San Miniato and the crossroads at the bottom turn right. After 150m turn left on the stepped lane of Via di San Salvatore del Monte. This climbs past Stations of the Cross to Viale Galileo Galilei.

Turn left for Piazzale Michelangelo, a fine but often busy viewpoint. Turn right; after some 50m steps and terraces lead off left to San Miniato al Monte. The 11th-century marble-clad church is worth a visit, and the views from here are also good if Piazzale Michelangelo below is rather crowded.

Distance
2km

Time
45 minutes or 2–3 hours with visits to churches, Museo Bardini and Forte del Belvedere

Start point
Ponte Vecchio
✚ 28C2

End point
San Miniato al Monte
✚ 29E1

Lunch
Cafés and restaurants with views on Viale Galileo Galilei, between Piazzale Michelangelo and San Miniato al Monte

Santa Felicita
✉ Piazza Santa Felicita
☎ 055/213 018
🕐 Daily 8–12, 3:30–6:30
♿ None
🎟 Free

Forte di Belvedere
✉ Costa di San Giorgio–Via di Belvedere
☎ 055/234 2822
🕐 Daily 9–dusk
♿ None
🎟 Free except during temporary exhibitions

Food & Drink

Poverty and peasant traditions have long inspired Tuscan cooking, with the result that the region's cuisine relies on simple, fresh ingredients and straightforward preparation and presentation. Simplicity is the key-note of most *antipasti*, (starters), which include hams, salamis and *crostini* (small rounds of toasted bread with mushroom, olive, chicken liver and other pâté-like toppings).

Local specialities make ideal presents

Typical first courses (*primi*) are *pappardelle alla lepre* (noodles in a hare sauce); *pici*, a Sienese pasta; vegetable-based *minestrone*; *pappa al pomodoro*, a tomato and basil soup thickened with bread; *risotto*, often with the region's prized *porcini* mushrooms; and *ribollita*, a soup of beans, cabbage, vegetables and bread. Beans are so ubiquitous in the region's cuisine – notably in *zuppa di fagioli* – that other Italians lampoon the Tuscans as *mangiafagioli* (bean-eaters).

Main Courses

Meat and fish (on the coast) provide the centrepiece of most main courses (*secondi*). The best-known dish is the majestic *bistecca alla fiorentina*, a large T-bone steak drizzled with olive oil, seasoned with herbs and grilled over the embers of a chestnut-wood fire. Other grilled meats (*alla griglia*) are also common, especially lamb (*agnello*), pork (*maiale*) and chicken (*pollo*). Game and wild boar (*cinghiale*) are often available. A mixed grill is known as *arrosto misto*; a casserole-type sauce of meat, tomatoes and olives is known as *alla cacciatore* ('hunter-style'). Tuscan *scottiglia* is a stew of poultry, white wine and veal (*vitello*).

Puddings

Puddings can disappoint in restaurants, often because they are made off the premises or laced with a virulent liqueur. Most Tuscans plump for fresh fruit (*frutta fresca*) – grapes, strawberries, cherries – or stroll to a *gelateria* for an ice-cream. Specialities include: *cantuccini*, almond biscuits dipped in dessert wine, or Siena's famous *panforte*, a combination of nuts and candied fruit. Cheese (*formaggio*) is also a good bet, especially sheep's cheese (*pecorino*).

Wine

Once upon a time Tuscan wine began and ended with Chianti. These days the region's wines are undergoing a renaissance, with many producers beginning to concentrate on high quality (and high-priced) wines. The grading system (DOC) is slightly discredited; many producers make wine independently, outside classification, known as *Vino da Tavola* and often better than DOC wine. Many are also experimenting with new grape varieties, blending French imports such as Cabernet Sauvignon with local staples such as Sangiovese (the grape used to make Chianti). *Sassicaia*, *Tignanello* and *Carmignano* are the best known of these 'Super Tuscans'.

Chianti is still the region's most famous wine, though two other great names offer more rewarding tipples if you can afford them: Brunello, from the area around Montalcino, is one of Italy's most majestic wines, produced by a bewildering array of tiny vineyards clustered around the ancient hill town. Its younger cousin, Rosso di Montalcino, is a cheaper but still outstanding alternative. Names to look out for include *Carpazo*, *Castello Romitorio* and the reasonably priced *Il Poggione*. Tuscany's other great wine is *Vino Nobile*, the ancient 'king of wines', produced around Montepulciano by estates such as Cantucci, Poliziano and Vecchia Cantina.

Reds have traditionally overshadowed the region's whites, the exceptions being *Galestro*, a light generic wine made by several producers, and *Vernaccia di San Gimignano*, which for years suffered a catastrophic fall in quality and prestige, and is now making a come-back. Most *Vernaccia* sold in San Gimignano's shops, however, is insipid plonk. If you want quality go for wines from Guicciardini's Cusona estate, makers of *Vernaccia* for 500 years, Teruzzi & Puthod's *Carmen* and *Terra di Tufo*, and Falchini's *Casale* and *Vigna a Solatio*.

In October rural Tuscany is alive with the sights and sounds of the grape harvest

🚩 29D4
✉ Piazza del Duomo 9
☎ 055/230 2885
🕓 Apr–Oct: Mon–Sat
9–6:50, Nov–Mar:
Mon–Sat 9–5:20. Closed
Sun and 1 Jan, Easter
Sun, 1 May, 15 Aug, 1
Nov, 8 Dec, 25–6 Dec
🍴 Near by (£)
🚌 1, 6, 7, 11, 14, 23
♿ Good to ground floor only
💶 Expensive
↔ Bargello (► 22),
Battistero (► 32),
Campanile (► 33),
Duomo (► 36–7)

MUSEO DELL'OPERA DEL DUOMO ✪✪✪

The Opera del Duomo was established in 1296 to supervise construction and maintenance of the cathedral and its many works of art. Today its sculpture collection ranks second only to the Bargello, having long housed artefacts removed for safe-keeping from the Duomo, Baptistery and Campanile. The ground floor features rooms filled with tools and models used during the Duomo's construction, together with sculpture removed from Arnolfo di Cambio's unfinished cathedral façade (demolished in 1587). Highlights from the latter include Donatello's *St John*, the thick-set *Madonna of the Glass Eyes* and the stiff-backed figure of *Pope Boniface VIII*. Donatello insisted on having a lock put on his workshop here, after a rival sculptor had sneaked in to see his work in progress. Another large room features models (1588) for the cathedral façade (none were ever realised); several illustrated volumes of choral music; and an octagonal chapel containing reliquaries and a lovely 14th-century altarpiece (1334).

The stairs to the next floor feature Michelangelo's outstanding *Pietà* (1550), a fitting prelude to two superlative *cantorie*, or carved choir lofts, which dominate the floor's opening room. The loft on the left (1431–8), carved in white marble, is by Luca della Robbia, that on the right (1433–9), with a far more dramatic arrangement by Donatello. Below the latter stands Donatello's extraor-

A piece of Roman sculpture in the courtyard of the Museo dell'Opera

dinary *Mary Magdalene*, while ranged around the walls are 16 statues removed from the Campanile. The room to the left features many age-blackened reliefs, also from the Campanile. The first floor's highlights, however, are the bronze panels crafted by Ghiberti for the Battistero doors, the centrepiece of a room crammed with paintings, mosaics and a glorious altarpiece (1459) by Antonio Pollaiuolo.

MUSEO DI SAN MARCO (► 23, TOP TEN)

MUSEO DI STORIA DELLA SCIENZA ⊗⊗

Despite its fall from artistic grace after the Renaissance, Florence remained at the forefront of European science and learning, thanks to the work of men such as Galileo – born in nearby Pisa – and the enlightened patronage of rulers such as Ferdinand II and Cosimo II. This well-presented and unexpectedly fascinating museum captures the flavour of the times, each of the many rooms (over two floors) being devoted to a separate scientific theme or discipline.

✚ 29D2
✉ Piazza dei Giudici
☎ 055/293 493
🕐 Tue, Thu, Sat, Sun 9:30–1, Mon, Wed, Fri 9:30–1, 2–5. Closed Sun and 1 Jan, 25 Apr, 1 May, 24 Jun, 15 Aug, 1 Nov, 8 Dec, 25–6 Dec
🍴 Near by (£)

The first floor opens with rooms devoted to counting machines and small instruments, including a case containing compasses which belonged to Michelangelo. Room 2's highlight is a beautifully enamelled quadrant; Room 3's is a lovely Tuscan astrolabe, two among hundreds of artefacts which display the Florentines' ability to turn even utilitarian objects into works of art. Room 4 features exhibits connected with Galileo, including the lens he used to discover the moons of Jupiter and – more bizarrely – some of the scientist's bones. Room 7, with its beautiful maps and globes, is one of the museum's loveliest corners.

The old microscopes of Room 9 lead to a salon devoted to the world's first scientific academy, the Accademia del Cimento, the body which – along with the Medici – was responsible for accumulating most of the museum's collection. Upstairs the museum delves into the mysteries of time and magnetism, followed by a sequence of less interesting pneumatic and hydrostatic displays. The best is saved until last: a roomful of alarming surgical instruments and horrifying anatomical waxworks.

🚌 23
♿ Excellent
💰 Expensive
↔ Uffizi (➤ 26), Ponte Vecchio (➤ 52)
❓ Loan of excellent free guides to each floor available on request (in four languages, including English)

Behind its austere façade the Museo di Storia della Scienza is one of Florence's most fascinating museums

✚ 29D3

✉ Orsanmichele: Via dei
Calzaiuoli (main entrance
to rear on Via dell'Arte
della Lana). Museum: Via
dell'Arte della Lana
(opposite church
entrance)

☎ 055/284 715

🕐 Church: 9–12, 4–6.
Museum: Mon–Sat 9–12,
Sun 9–12:30

🍴 Near by (£)

🚌 In the pedestrian zone:
nearest services 1, 6, 7,
11, 14, 23

♿ Church: good. Museum:
none

🎟 Free

↔ Battistero (➤ 32),
Campanile (➤ 33),
Duomo (➤ 36–7), Palazzo
Vecchio (➤ 50), Piazza
della Signoria (➤ 51)

ORSANMICHELE ✪✪

Orsanmichele is one of Florence's most intimate churches, providing a calm retreat from the crowds of Via dei Calzaiuoli. The site's earliest church dates from 750, a small chapel situated in the kitchen garden (*orto*) of a Benedictine monastery. From these humble roots came its present name, which is a contraction of *San Michele ad Hortum* and *San Michele in Orto*. In 1280 the chapel was replaced with a grain market, a building destroyed by fire in 1304. In 1380 this was replaced with another church, the upper floor being retained as a granary.

Decoration of the new building was entrusted to the city's leading guilds, each of which was asked to commission a statue of its patron saint to adorn the exterior. After years of delays, statues were eventually secured from some of the greatest Renaissance artists, among them Verrocchio, Ghiberti, Donatello and Giambologna.

Some of these statues, such as Donatello's *St George,* have now been replaced with copies, the originals removed for safe-keeping to the church museum and other city galleries. Others occupy their original niches, and have been cleaned as part of a large restoration programme. The interior, however, retains many of its oldest treasures, not least a magnificent glass and marble tabernacle (1348–59) by Andrea Orcagna, a work financed by votive offerings which flooded in after the Black Death of 1348. At its heart is a *Madonna and Child* (1347), a painting which is said to have inherited the miracle-working properties of a fresco on the site, destroyed in the fire of 1304. Most of the interior's frescoes, which were painted to complement the exterior sculptures, show the guild's patron saints.

The Madonna and Child *at the heart of Andrea Orcagna's sumptuous tabernacle*

PALAZZO MEDICI-RICCARDI ✪✪✪

To the average bystander this palace looks like just one more grime-covered Florentine *palazzo*. Built for Cosimo de' Medici in 1444, it was designed by Michelozzo, the Medici's leading architect, and remained the family's main home until Cosimo I moved to the Palazzo Vecchio in 1540. Its heavily rusticated ground-floor exterior, almost fortress-like in appearance, was to influence many Florentine buildings in the century of palace-building which followed. Today much of the mansion is occupied by council offices, making the survival of one of the city's most charming fresco cycles all the more remarkable.

Benozzo Gozzoli painted the three-panel *Journey of the Magi* (1459) for Piero de' Medici, probably in honour of the Compagnia dei Magi, one of the city's leading religious confraternities (of which the Medici were leading members). Tucked away in the tiny Cappella dei Magi, the cycle has recently been restored to stunning effect. The three principal panels deal with one of the three kings of the Nativity, though most interest derives from Gozzoli's inclusion of contemporary portraits among the sea of faces. On the right wall, for example, the long procession is headed by a courtly figure probably intended to represent Lorenzo the Magnificent.

Did you know ?

Gozzoli included a self-portrait in the right hand wall fresco. He stands a couple of rows from the rear of the procession with the words OPUS BENOTI picked out in gold on his red hat.

🏠 29D5

✉ Via Cavour 1–2

☎ 055/276 0340 or 276 0526

🕐 Mon, Tue, Thu–Sat 9–1, 3–6, Sun and public hols 9–1

🍴 Near by (£)

🚌 1, 6, 7

♿ None: several flights of stairs

💵 Palace exterior and courtyard: free. Cappella dei Magi: moderate (tickets from the office in walled garden through courtyard)

↔ Michelangelo's *David* (➤ 19), Battistero (➤ 32), Campanile (➤ 33), Duomo (➤ 36–7), Museo dell'Opera del Duomo (➤ 44), San Lorenzo (➤ 54–5)

❓ The Cappella dei Magi is reached by taking the first doorway on the right off the courtyard (with your back to the place entrance) and climbing the stairs to the second floor

A sumptuous ceiling within the Palazzo Medici-Riccardi

PALAZZO PITTI

Palaces and galleries do not come much larger than the Palazzo Pitti, home to the Medici for some 200 years and now the setting for much of their private collection of paintings, silverware, costumes and miscellaneous objets d'art. The palace was begun in 1457 by Luca Pitti, a wealthy banker (possibly to a design by Brunelleschi), partly to upstage the Medici, then the Pitti's implacable rivals. By 1549 the Pitti had fallen on hard times, forcing them – ironically – to sell up to their old rivals. Once installed, the Medici altered the palace beyond recognition, adding two vast wings and countless additional rooms and salons.

These now house four separate museums, whose layout can be slightly confusing. The main thing to see is the Galleria Palatina, home to a superlative collection of paintings (its entrance is to the rear right-hand side of the courtyard and up the stairs to the second floor). Within the Galleria, which is also something of a maze, you should start with the Sala di Venere (Room 1), work down the following five state rooms, then return along the smaller parallel rooms to your starting point. The ceiling fresco in the Sala di Venere is the first of four, all by Piero da Cortona, each depicting allegorical and mythological scenes inspired by the Medici. The room also contains the first of the gallery's many exceptional paintings, which here (as elsewhere) are wedged from floor to ceiling with little attempt at classification. Critics often complain at the arrangement and poor labelling, though this provides a vivid illustration of the collection's size, and is how the Medici Grand Dukes chose to display their paintings.

Room 2, the Sala di Apollo, contains one of the gallery's many masterpieces, Titian's *Portrait of a Gentleman* (1540), along with the same artist's sensuous *Mary Magdalene* (1531) and Van Dyck's portraits of *Charles I and Henrietta Maria*. The next room, the Sala di Marte, features Rubens' huge *Consequences of War* (1638), an allegory of the Thirty Years' War. The next room, the Sala di Giove, was once the grand-ducal throne room. Today it is home to one of Raphael's finest portraits, the *Donna Velata*, (*Veiled Woman*, 1516). More Raphaels line the walls of the next two rooms, including the famous *Madonna della Seggiola* (1515), along with works by Andrea del Sarto, Tintoretto, Giorgione, Perugino, Velázquez and others. Highlights of the parallel rooms include Crisofano Allori's celebrated *Judith and Holofernes*, Caravaggio's *Sleeping Cupid* and a sublime *Madonna and Child* by Filippo Lippi.

The most worthwhile of the Pitti's other museums is the Museo degli Argenti, whose lavish salons display the silverware, *pietra dura* vases and other priceless (if often tasteless) artefacts accumulated by the Medici. The Galleria d'Arte Moderna contains some 30 rooms of Tuscan paintings (1784–1945), the most interesting of which are by the *Macchiaioli* group, often called the Italian Impressionists. The Galleria del Costume has a sumptuous collection of clothes and costumes from the heyday of the Medici court.

The Palazzo Pitti contains countless sublime paintings and gloriously decorated rooms

+ 29D2
✉ Piazza della Signoria
☎ 055/276 8465
🕐 Mon–Wed, Fri, Sat 9–7,
Sun and public hols 8–1.
Last admission 1 hour
before closing. Closed
Thu and 1 Jan, Easter
Sun, 1 May, 15 Aug,
25–6 Dec
🍴 Near by (£)
🚌 In the pedestrian zone:
nearest services 19, 23,
31, 32
♿ Good
💷 Expensive
↔ Uffizi (► 26),
Orsanmichele (► 46),
Piazza della Signoria
(► 51)
❓ In summer tours are
sometimes organised to
parts of the palace
normally closed to
visitors: consult tourist
office for details

*The Palazzo Vecchio's
lovely courtyard was
designed by Michelozzo
and decorated by Vasari*

PALAZZO VECCHIO ★★

The Palazzo Vecchio (c1285–1322) served as Florence's official seat of government for about seven centuries – (it's still the town hall.) Designed by Arnolfo di Cambio, then also employed on the Duomo, it was finished in 1303, but radically altered by Cosimo I in 1540 when he moved the Medici court here from the Palazzo Medici-Riccardi. When Cosimo moved again in 1550, this time to the 'new' Palazzo Pitti, the palace took its present name (*vecchio* means 'old').

Its courtyard (1453) was designed by Michelozzo, one of the Medici's favourite architects, and later adorned by Vasari with decorative paens to Medici prowess. Vasari also built the staircase which leads to the palace's focal point, the vast but soulless Salone dei Cinquecento, built in 1495 to accommodate the 500 members of Florence's ruling assembly. Vasari decorated both its ceiling – whose gilt-laden paintings glorify Cosimo I – and the walls, whose six huge paintings (1563–5) depict a succession of Florentine military triumphs. Beneath them may be a series of unfinished frescoes begun in 1506 by Michelangelo and Leonardo.

A statue of *Victory* (1525) by Michelangelo stands almost opposite the Salone's entrance, while just off the chamber is the tiny Studiolo (entrance door wall), a tiny but exquisitely decorated room designed for Francesco I, Cosimo's gloomy son. On the second floor enjoy the view from the Terrazza di Saturno, the many decorated rooms – notably Bronzino's Mannerist chapel – and the view of the Piazza della Signoria from the Sala d'Udienza. The Sala dei Gigli contains frescoes by Domenico Ghirlandaio and Donatello's statue of *Judith and Holofernes*, widely considered the palace's masterpiece.

PIAZZA DELLA SIGNORIA ✪✪

While the Piazza del Duomo was Florence's religious focus, the Piazza della Signoria has long served as the city's civic and political heart. Witness to countless momentous events across the centuries, such as the burning of Savonarola in 1498, it remains one of the city's busiest meeting places, and the natural conclusion of the evening *passeggiata* (stroll) along Via dei Calzaiuoli. It was first enlarged in 1307 to accommodate the Palazzo dei Priori (now the Palazzo Vecchio), and was paved as early as 1385.

Sights include the Palazzo Vecchio, the Uffizi (off the square to the south), and the Loggia dei Lanzi, an outdoor gallery sheltering several outstanding pieces of sculpture. Greatest of these are Cellini's *Perseus* (1554) and Giambologna's contorted *Rape of the Sabine Women* (1583), though there are plans to replace these and other of the loggia's sculptures with copies.

More statues adorn the piazza itself: from left to right as you face the Palazzo Vecchio they include Giambologna's equestrian statue of *Cosimo I* (1587–94); the Neptune Fountain (1563–75) by Ammananti (the central figure of which was ridiculed by Michelangelo);next the *Marzocco*, a copy of Donatello's Florentine heraldic lion; *Judith and Holofernes* (1456–60), a copy of Donatello's statue in the Palazzo Vecchio; *David*, an 1873 copy of Michelangelo's most famous sculpture; and Bandinelli's *Hercules and Cacus* (1534), a work intended to symbolise Cosimo I, Florentine fortitude and the defeat of domestic enemies. On its unveiling the work was described by a fellow sculptor as a 'sack of melons'.

✚	29D3
✉	Piazza della Signoria
☎	None
⏰	Daily, 24 hours
🍴	Rivoire (▶ 57)
🚌	In the pedestrian zone: nearest services 19, 23, 31, 32
♿	Good
✋	Free
↔	Uffizi (▶ 26), Palazzo Vecchio (▶ 50)

Copies of famous sculptures stare down on Piazza della Signoria

🗺 28C2
✉ Ponte Vecchio
☎ None
🕐 Daily, 24 hours
🍴 Near by (£–££)
🚶 Pedestrianised
♿ Good
💷 Free
↔ Uffizi (► 26), Museo della Antica Casa Fiorentina (► 39), Palazzo Pitti (► 48), Palazzo Vecchio (► 50), Piazza della Signoria (► 51)
❓ Corridoio Vasariano occasionally open to visitors: consult Uffizi or tourist office for current opening times

PONTE VECCHIO ✪✪✪

The Ponte Vecchio and its huddle of old buildings are among the most familiar sights of Florence. Pitched close to the Arno's narrowest point, this is the last in a long succession of bridges on the site, dating back to Roman times. In 1944 it was the only Florentine bridge spared by the retreating Nazis, reputedly saved on Hitler's direct orders. In 1966 it was spared again – just – when it withstood the flood which brought death and destruction to much of Florence.

Until 1218 the bridge was the city's only river crossing, providing a vital lifeline between the old centre and the Oltrarno, on the Arno's southern bank. The present structure, which dates from 1345, was built to replace a bridge swept away in the floods of 1333 (some of the worst in the city's history). Its name ('Old Bridge') was coined to distinguish it from the Arno's other bridge, the Ponte alla Carraia, originally built in 1218.

Shops first appeared on the bridge during the 14th century, most of them butchers and fishmongers attracted by the river, a convenient dumping ground for offal and other refuse. The next arrivals were the tanners, who soaked hides in the river before adding to the communal stench by tanning them with horse's urine. Across the top of the shops runs the Corridoio Vasariano, built by Vasari to enable Cosimo I to walk undisturbed between his home (the Palazzo Vecchio) and offices (the Uffizi). In 1593 Ferdinand I raised shop rents and decreed that only jewellers and goldsmiths should occupy the bridge. They remain to this day.

The famous Ponte Vecchio has stood on the River Arno since 1345

Santissima Annunziata's inner courtyard, the Chiostro dei Voti, is swathed in Renaissance frescoes

SANTISSIMA ANNUNZIATA ⭐

The church of SS Annunziata lies on one of Florence's lesser-known but most architecturally pleasing squares. Laid out by Brunelleschi in the 1420s, the area was altered several times over the next 200 years, the most notable additions being Giambologna's equestrian statue of Ferdinand I (1608) and two bizarre little fountains, the work of Giambologna's pupil, Pietro Tacca.

The church, which dominates the piazza's northern flanks, was built to honour the Annunciation, a crucial event in the life of the city: in the old Florentine calendar, the New Year began on the Feast of the Annunciation (25 March). It is now the mother church of the Servites, an order founded in 1234 by would-be servants (*servi*) of the Virgin.

The order built a chapel, which began drawing the crowds after 1252, when a painting begun by a Servite monk was miraculously completed by an angel. By 1450 so many pilgrims were coming that a new church, paid for by the Medici, was commissioned to house the painting. Via dei Servi was built at the same time to link SS Annunziata and the Duomo, the two most important churches in the city dedicated to the Virgin.

The church's main sight is the inner courtyard, the Chiostro dei Voti (1447), swathed in frescoes by Andrea del Sarto, Jacopo Pontormo and Rosso Fiorentino. Inside the main body of the church lies Michelozzo's magnificent Tempietto (1448–61), built to shelter the miraculous painting. The first two chapels on the left feature celebrated works by Andrea del Castagno.

SANTA CROCE (▶ 24, TOP TEN)

- 29E5
- ✉ Piazza della Santissima Annunziata
- ☎ 055/210 644 or 239 8034
- 🕐 Daily 7–12, 4–6:30
- 🍽 Near by
- 🚌 6, 31, 32
- ♿ Good 🅿 Free
- ↔ *David*, Galleria dell'Accademia (▶ 19), Museo di San Marco (▶ 23), Palazzo Medici-Riccardi (▶ 47)
- ❓ The eastern side of Piazza della SS Annunziata is dominated by a loggia (1493) built by Brunelleschi for the **Ospedale degli Innocenti**, Europe's first orphanage. The Ospedale's small Renaissance art collection and contrasting 'Men's' and 'Women's' cloisters are open to the public

Ospedale degli Innocenti

- ✉ Piazza della Santissima Annunziata
- ☎ 055/247 9317
- 🕐 Mon, Tue, Thu–Sat 8:30–2, Sun and public hols 8:30–1. Closed 1 Jan, Easter Sun, 1 May, 15 Aug, 25–6 Dec
- 🅿 Moderate

29C5

Piazza San Lorenzo

San Lorenzo: 055/216
634. Biblioteca
Laurenziana: 055/214 443
or 210 760

San Lorenzo: daily 7–12,
3:30–6. Biblioteca
Laurenziana: Mon–Sat
9–1

Near by (£)

In the pedestrian zone

Few

Free

Cappelle Medicee
(➤ 17), Battistero (➤ 32),
Campanile (➤ 33),
Duomo (➤ 36–7),
Palazzo Medici-Riccardi
(➤ 47)

SAN LORENZO ✪✪✪

San Lorenzo was founded in 393, making it one of the oldest churches in Florence. It served as the city's cathedral until the 7th century. A Romanesque church built on the site in 1060 survived until 1419, when Giovanni de' Medici and a group of parishioners offered to pay for a new church. Brunelleschi, then working on the Duomo, started work two years later, but progress faltered in the face of political and financial upheavals, and only resumed when Giovanni's son, Cosimo de' Medici, offered 40,000 florins to ensure its completion (150 florins at this time could support a family for a year). As a result, the church became the Medici's dynastic church, while its rear portion, the Cappelle Medicee, became their private chapel (➤ 17).

The interior is an early Renaissance masterpiece. Brunelleschi created 'sails' of creamy wall interspersed with austere grey *pietra serena*. Artistic highlights include Rosso Fiorentino's *Marriage of the Virgin* (second altar on the right) and Desiderio da Settignano's *Pala del Sacramento* (1451–68), on the wall at the end of the right nave.

In the centre of the church stand two raised pulpits (1455–66), among the last works of Donatello (and pupils), and in front of the high altar brass grilles mark the tomb of Cosimo de' Medici (with a plaque inscribed *Pater Patriae* –

Father of the Fatherland). The *Martyrdom of St Laurence* (1565–9), left of the two pulpits, is a graphic painting by Bronzino. In a chapel round the corner is a cenotaph to Donatello, who died in 1464 and was buried near Cosimo, his friend and patron. Brunelleschi's Sagrestia Vecchia, or Old Sacristy (1421), a simple architectural gem, is entered from the left transept of the church. On the left as you enter stands the bronze and porphyry tomb of Giovanni and Piero de' Medici (Cosimo de' Medici's sons), and in the centre is the tomb of Giovanni and Piccarda, Cosimo's parents and founders of the Medici fortune.

Most of the sacristy's decoration (1434–43) is by Donatello, most notably the eight *tondi* showing the Evangelists and scenes from the life of St John (Giovanni's patron saint). The reliefs above the doors of the end wall portray Cosmos and Damian, the Medici's patron saints, and saints Laurence and Stephen, protectors of Florence.

From the church cloisters, stairs lead to the Biblioteca Laurenziana,

Did you know ?

St Laurence (San Lorenzo), was a 3rd-century Roman martyr, roasted alive on a grid-iron because when the Romans had ordered him to collect 'all the treasures of the Church', Laurence had gathered all the sick and poor people he could find. During his roasting he apparently told his tormentors they could turn him over: 'I am done on this side'.

begun in 1524 to house the Medici's vast 100-year old library, collected by agents sent as far afield as Germany and the Middle East. Michelangelo designed the Ricetto (Vestibule), with its revolutionary use of space, and almost every detail of the library Reading Room – even the desks. The four rooms beyond contain a fraction of the books and manuscripts.

Above: *Statues by Michelangelo in the Cappelle Medicee*
Left: *The cloisters of San Lorenzo*

In the Know

If you only have a short time to visit Tuscany and Florence, or want to get a real flavour of the region, here are some ideas:

10
Ways To Be A Local

Join the evening *passeggiata* (stroll) in Via dei Calzaiuoli.

Drink espresso after lunch or dinner – the Italians *never* have cappuccino with a meal.

Visit *Vivoli* at Via Isola delle Stinche 7r for the best ice-cream in Florence (see below).

Buy your stationery from *Pineider* in Piazza della Signoria.

Join the locals on Sunday to watch Fiorentina, Florence's *Serie* A soccer team.

Take an afternoon siesta on hot summer afternoons.

Don't make a *brutta figura* – an 'ugly image' or fool of yourself – by dressing badly or drinking too much.

Take a Sunday morning stroll in the Giardino di Boboli.

Make an extra effort with your appearance when you're dining out.

Do your shopping in the old Mercato Centrale.

10
Good Places to Have Lunch

Antellesi (£–££) ✉ Via Faenza 9r ☎ 055/216 990: an easy-going place with simple wooden tables and traditional dishes.

Belle Donne (£–££) ✉ Via delle Belle Donne 16r ☎ 055/238 2609: a tiny and genial restaurant with shared tables and eye-catching décor.

Cantinetta Antinori (££) ✉ Piazza Antinori 3 ☎ 055/292 234: elegant and beautiful wine bar with a lively atmosphere.

Cantinetta dei Verrazzano (££) ✉ Via dei Tavolini 18–20r ☎ 055/268 590: nice wine bar with marble-topped tables and tasty Tuscan snacks.

Casalinga (£) ✉ Via dei Michelozzi 9r ☎ 055/218 624: authentic Oltrarno trattoria, popular with locals and visitors alike.

Cibreo (££) ✉ Via del Verrocchio 8 118r ☎ 055/234 1100: have lunch in the cheaper bistro to the rear of the main restaurant.

Da Ganino (£–££) ✉ Piazza dei Cimatori 4r ☎ 055/214 125: central, reasonably priced restaurant with outside tables.

Il Cantinone del Gallo Nero (£) ✉ Via Santo Spirito 6r ☎ 055/218 898: wine bar in vaulted cellar with a choice of starters and hot and cold snacks.

Latini (£) ✉ Via dei Palchetti, off Via della Vigna Nuova ☎ 055/210 916: a busy trattoria with crowded tables and raucous atmosphere.

Le Volpi e L'Uva (£–££) ✉ Piazza dei Rossi 1r serve Florence's best ☎ 055/239 8132: a refined and delightful wine bar with a wide variety of wines and cold snacks.

10
Good Places for Snacks, Coffee or Cakes

Cennini (£) ✉ Borgo San Jacopo 51r ☎ 055/ 294 930: lots of delicious home-made cakes: the *torta della nonna* is particularly renowned.

Daria (£) Borgo degli Albizi 36r ☎ 055/234 0979: a third generation family-run bar and Florentine institution dating from the 1940s.

Giacosa (££) Via dei Tornabuoni 83r ☎ 055/239 6226: sophisticated 19th-century bar where the Negroni cocktail was born: also renowned for its marrons glacés and other confectionery.

Gilli (££) Via Roma 1r–Piazza della Repubblica 39r ☎ 055/239 6310: Florence's oldest and grandest bar; the most tempting of the four famous cafés on Piazza della Repubblica.

Giubbe Rosse (££) Piazza della Repubblica 13–14r ☎ 055/212 280: celebrated 19th-century literary café; one of Piazza della Repubblica's 'Big Four' bars.

Manaresi (£) Via de' Lamberti 16r ☎ None: thought by many to serve Florence's best cup of coffee.

Pasticceria Robiglio (£) Via dei Servi 112r ☎ 055/212 784 or 214 501 Via Tosingi ☎ 055/215 013: a family-run Florence institution founded in the 1920s: its two outlets sell some of the city's best cakes and confectionery.

Paszkowski (££) Piazza della Repubblica 6r ☎ 055/210 236: venerable and much feted Piazza della Repubblica café.

Procacci (£–££) Via dei Tornabuoni 64r ☎ 055/211 656: smart bar known for its legendary *panini tartufati* – truffle purée sandwiches.

Rivoire (££) Piazza della Signoria 5r ☎ 055/214 412: expensive and well-known bar with outside tables on the main square.

5
Good Places for Ice-Cream

Carabé (£) Via Ricasoli 60r ☎ 055/289 476: after seeing *David* in the Accademia, near by, come here for a *granita* (crushed ice with a choice of fruit syrup) or a tub of the excellent pistachio ice-cream.

Häagen-Daz (£) Piazza Signoria-Via Vacchereccia 3 ☎ 055/2282 986: it was something of a risk to bring a foreign name to the home of ice-cream, but the product is good even so.

Granduca (£) Via dei Calzaiuoli 57r: first stop for ice-cream on Florence's main Via dei Calzaiuoli.

Perchè No! (£) Via dei Tavolini 19r ☎ 055/239 8969: a central *gelateria* which has been in business since 1939.

Vivoli (£) Via Isole delle Stinche 7r ☎ 055/292 334: quiet simply the best ice-cream in Florence – perhaps even in Italy.

5
Best Tuscan Views

- From the Campanile, Florence.
- From the Torre del Mangia in the Palazzo Pubblico, Siena.
- From the walls of the hilltop village of Pienza.
- From the Torre dei Guinigi, Lucca.
- From the Torre Grossa, San Gimignano.

10
Top Activities

Canoeing: contact the Federazione Italiana Canoa, Borgo Ognissanti 39, 50123, Firenze (☎ 055/689 044).

Caving: excellent opportunities in the Alpi Apuane: contact the Gruppo Speleologico Fiorentino, Via Torre del Gallo 30, 50125, Florence (☎ 055/229 9979).

Cycling: bikes can be hired in Florence and most large towns. Contact individual tourist offices for details.

Diving: off the coast and islands of the Tuscan Archipelago: contact the Federazione Italiana Attività Subacquee (FIAS), Via Aurelia 640, 57012, Castiglioncello (LI), Tuscany.

Fishing: plenty of coastal and sea fishing. Contact local tourist offices for details of conditions, permits and tackle shops.

Horse-riding: riding and pony-trekking are widely available throughout Tuscany: most tourist offices carry lists of local centres.

Mountaineering: in the Alpi Apuane, Orecchiella and elsewhere. Most towns have a branch office of the Club Alpino Italiano (CAI): contact tourist offices for local addresses. The Florence office is at Via Studio 5 (☎ 055/211 731).

Skiing: winter sports are available, snow allowing, around Abetone, to the north east of Lucca.

Windsurfing: off the coast and islands of the Tuscan archipelago, notably Elba. Contact the Associazione Surfisti Italiani Versilia, Via Nino Bixio 30, 55049 Viareggio (LU), Tuscany.

Walking: for the best-organised accompanied and self-guided walking holidays in Tuscany contact the Alternative Travel Group, 69–71 Banbury Road, Oxford, UK (☎ 01865 310399).

🔲 28B4

✉ Piazza Santa Maria
   Novella

☎ 055/282 187 or 210 113

🕐 Santa Maria Novella:
   Mon–Sat 7–11:30,
   3:30–6, Sun and religious
   hols 8–12, 3:30–5.
   Museo di Santa Maria
   Novella: Mon–Thu, Sat
   9–2, Sun 8–1. Closed Fri
   and 1 Jan, Easter Sun, 25
   Apr, 1 May, 15 Aug, 25–6
   Dec

🍴 Near by in Piazza Santa
   Maria Novella (£)

🚌 All services to the railway
   station

♿ Good

🎟 Santa Maria Novella: free.
   Museo di Santa Maria
   Novella: moderate

↔ Cappelle Medicee
   (➤ 17), Santa Trinita
   (➤ 63)

❓ Guided tours of the
   church occasionally
   available

SANTA MARIA NOVELLA

Santa Maria Novella ranks second only to Santa Croce in the pantheon of great Florentine churches. Begun as a simple chapel in the 9th century, it was rebuilt in 1094 and christened Santa Maria delle Vigne (Mary of the Vineyards). It then passed to the Dominicans, who in 1246 began a new church. The Romanesque façade was not finished until 1456, when Leon Battista Alberti completed the multi-coloured frontage.

The lofty Gothic interior has several important frescoes, the most famous of which is Masaccio's *Trinità* (1428), mid-way down the left wall, one of the first Renaissance paintings to put the new theories of perspective to good use. Close by is Brunelleschi's pulpit (1443–52), where the Inquisition first denounced Galileo for agreeing with Copernicus that the earth revolved around the sun, and not vice versa.

Many of the church's chapels were commissioned by leading Renaissance businessmen. Banker Filippo Strozzi employed Filippino Lippi to fresco the Cappella di Filippo Strozzi with scenes from the life of his namesake, St Philip (Filippo) the Apostle. The chapel to its right, the Cappella Bardi, features faded 14th-century frescoes, some attributed to Cimabue, Giotto's first teacher.

To the left of the Strozzi chapel, in the chancel, is Domenico Ghirlandaio's beautiful fresco cycle on the *Life of the Virgin* (left wall) and *Life of St John the Baptist* (right wall). Despite their religious themes, these are actually vignettes of daily life in 15th-century Florence; they were commissioned by another banker, Giovanni Tornabuoni, whose relations appear in several scenes.

More frescoes (1351–7), the work of Nardo di Cione, adorn the Cappella Strozzi (up steps at the top left-hand side of the church): *Paradiso* (left wall), the *Last Judgement* (behind the altar), and a map-like *Inferno* (right wall), a commentary on Dante's epic poem *The Divine Comedy*. The altarpiece is by Nardo's brother, Andrea di Cione, better known as Orcagna, and shows *Christ Giving the Keys to St Peter and the Book of Knowledge to Thomas Aquinas* (the chapel is dedicated to Aquinas.

Left of Santa Maria's façade is the entrance to the church museum and Chiostro Verde (Green Cloister), named after the green pigment of its badly faded frescoes. Despite the deterioration, many of the panels are superb – especially Paolo Uccello's *Universal Deluge* (1430), whose lurching composition illustrates his obsession with perspective. Notice the arks to either side of the picture, depicted before and after the Flood.

Off the cloister lies the Cappellone degli Spagnuoli, once used by the Spanish entourage of Eleanor of Toledo, wife of Cosimo I. It features one of the city's most striking fresco cycles, the work of Andrea da Firenze.

The left wall shows *The Triumph of Doctrine*, with Thomas Aquinas enthroned amidst the Virtues and Doctors of the Church.

The right wall portrays *The Work and Triumph of the Dominican Order*, with St Dominic unleashing the 'hounds of the Lord' (*Domini canes*, a pun on 'Dominicans'. The four women are the Four Vices, surrounded by dancing and other debaucheries. A nearby friar hears confessions before sending the saved heavenwards; above the kneeling pilgrims are portraits of Dante, Petrarch, Giotto and others.

Santa Maria Novella's façade was completed 200 years after the church was begun

A Walk around Fiesole

Distance
2.5km one way

Time
Allow a morning

Start point
Piazza Mino da Fiesole
 65D5

End point
Badia Fiorentina or Piazza
Mino da Fiesole
65D5

ℹ️ Tourist office: Piazza
Mino da Fiesole 36–7
(☎ 055/598 720)

🚌 7 ATAF bus from
Florence railway station,
Piazza San Marco or Via
Martelli (near the Duomo)
to Piazza Mino da
Fiesole. Services call at
San Domenico di Fiesole,
near the Badia Fiesolana,
for the return to
Florence.

Lunch
Cafés around Piazza Mino
da Fiesole (£)

**Teatro Romano–Museo
Archeologico**
✉ Via Marini
☎ 055/59 477
🕐 Daily 9–dusk. Closed Tue
in winter
💰 Moderate
❓ Museum ticket includes
entrance to the
Antiquarium Costantini

Museo Bandini
✉ Via Dupré
☎ 055/59 477
🕐 May–Oct, Wed–Mon
9:30–1, 3–7; Oct–Apr,
10–1, 3–6
💰 Moderate
❓ Combined ticket available
with Antiquarium
Costantini

The ancient hill town of Fiesole nestles in the hills above
Florence, providing a tranquil retreat from the city during
the dog-days of summer. It is a popular destination at
weekends, so be prepared for crowds.

*Start in Piazza Mino da Fiesole and take Via
Marini to the right of the Duomo to the Museo
Bandini and archaeological zone.*

The Cappella Salutati in the Duomo features two works by
Mino da Fiesole: the *Tomb of Bishop Salutati* and an altar-
frontal of the *Madonna and Child.* The cathedral's high altar
has an impressive altarpiece by Bicci di Lorenzo. Off Via
Marini lie the 1st-century BC Teatro Romano, the Museo
Archeologico and the ruins of Etruscan walls and temples.
The Antiquarium Costantini, in Via Portigiani, contains a
fine collection of Greek vases. The Bandini museum
houses early Florentine paintings. There is a combined
museum ticket available which includes admission to the
Antiquarium Costantini.

*Return to Piazza Mino da Fiesole and take Via
San Francesco off its north–west flank. Walk
uphill to see San Francesco and Sant'Alessandro,
returning to the piazza the way you came or via
the parallel/nearby woodland path.*

Sant'Alessandro, one of the town's loveliest buildings, was
built in the 6th century over the site of Roman and
Etruscan temples. San Francesco enjoys breezy views of
Florence, and has an important 15th-century painting, *The
Immaculate Conception,* by Piero di Cosimo.

*From the Piazza take Via Vecchia Fiesolana
past the Villa Medici to San Domenico. Turn
right on Via Badia dei Roccettini to the Badia
Fiesolana.*

San Domenico contains a *Madonna and Child with Angels*
(1430) by Fra Angelico; the chapter house (number 4)
has a *Crucifixion* by the same artist. The Badia features a
lovely 11th-centuthy façade incorporated into a 15th-
century frontage. Its interior is styled in the manner of
Brunelleschi. This was Fiesole's original cathedral.

*Tranquil Fiesole nestles in the hills above Florence, providing
suberb views across the city*

🕀 29E1
✉ Off Viale Galileo Galilei
☎ 055/234 2731
🕐 Daily 8–12, 2–6
🍴 Near by in Viale Galileo
    Galilei (£–££)
🚍 12, 13
♿ Good, but steps to parts
    of church
🎫 Free

SAN MINIATO AL MONTE ✪✪✪

The most beautiful church in Florence takes its name from St Minias, an Oriental Christian merchant who was martyred in Florence in AD 250. According to legend the saint picked up his severed head and carried it from his place of execution (close to Piazza della Signoria) across the Arno to the hilltop site where his church now stands. Most of the present building dates from 1013, making it among the city's oldest churches.

The Romanesque façade (1090–1270) features a mosaic of Christ, Mary and St Minias (1260) and a gilded eagle clasping a bale of wool – symbol of the Arte di Calimala, the wealthy guild which was made responsible for the church's fabric in 1228.

The breathtaking interior is dominated by a sumptuous painted wooden ceiling (1322) and a famous inlaid pavement (1207), reputedly inspired by Sicilian fabrics, and patterned with lions, doves and the signs of the zodiac. The capitals on the pillars of the nave are Roman and Byzantine originals. In the left-hand aisle is the Cappella del Cardinale del Portogallo, a Renaissance masterpiece complete with paintings, glazed terracotta and funerary sculpture, the works of sculptor Antonio Rossellino and painters Baldovinetti and two brothers, Antonio and Pietro Pollaiuolo. The Cardinal of Portugal, whose uncle was King of Portugal died in Florence in 1459. At the end of the nave, alongside Michelozzo's free-standing Cappella del Crocifisso (1448), steps lead to the raised choir and a magnif-

Part of San Miniato's breathtaking interior

icent carved pulpit and screen (1207). The sacristy, off to the right boasts a vivid fresco cycle by Spinello Aretino depicting *Scenes from the Life of St Benedict* (1387).

Santa Trínita's distinctive baroque façade masks a more austere Gothic interior

SANTA TRÍNITA ★

Santa Trínita is something of an architectural curiosity. Its flamboyant baroque exterior makes a striking contrast with the calm, Gothic assurance of its interior. Founded in 1092, it was rebuilt between 1258 and 1280 – possibly to a design by Nicola Pisano – and the façade was added by Buontalenti in 1593.

The dusky, atmospheric interior has several wonderful works of art, most notably Domenico Ghirlandaio's frescoes (1483) in the Cappella Sassetti (the right-hand chapel to the right of the high altar). They represent episodes from the life of St Francis, and were commissioned by Francesco Sassetti in a bid to outdo his rival, Francesco Tornabuoni, who had paid for the frescoes in Santa Maria Novella, also by Ghirlandaio.

The panel portraying *St Francis Receiving the Rule* in the lunette above the altar is famous for its setting – the Piazza della Signoria – and its portraits, which include Sassetti, who worked for the Medici bank, between his son, Federigo, and Lorenzo the Magnificent. On the stairs stand the humanist Poliziano and three of his pupils, the sons of Lorenzo the Magnificent.

The chapel's altarpiece, also by Ghirlandaio (1485), depicts *The Adoration of the Magi,* combining classical and Christian motifs (notice the Roman sarcophagus). Sassetti and his wife are portrayed to either side. Other works of art include Lorenzo Monaco's early 15th-century frescoes (fourth chapel on the right), the *Tomb of Bishop Federighi* (1454–7) by Luca della Robbia (second chapel left of the altar), and frescoes by Neri di Bicci and Bicci di Lorenzo (fourth chapel on the left).

UFFIZI, GALLERIA DEGLI (➤ 26, TOP TEN)

✠ 28B3
✉ Piazza di Santa Trínita
☎ 055/216 912
🕓 Daily 9–11:30, 4–5:30.
Summer hours may be longer
🍴 Near by (£)
🚌 6, 11, 31, 32, 36, 37
♿ Good
🎫 Free
↔ Museo della Antica Casa Fiorentina (➤ 39), Ponte Vecchio (➤ 52), Santa Maria Novella (➤ 58–9)

TOSCANA

0   20   40 km

A   B   C

Tuscany

Tuscany is Italy at its best, a region of lovely medieval hilltowns, sleepy villages and cypress-ringed villas and farmhouses. Vineyards, olives and fields of sunflowers mingle with rambling wooded hills, ragged mountains and sun-baked plains to form landscapes of timeless beauty. Art and culture are everywhere, from dusty Madonnas in half-forgotten churches to frescoes in majestic hill-top monasteries. And then there's the food and wine – as alluring as any number of paintings and hilltop towns.

Siena is the region's premier town, home to some of the most attractive medieval streets, museums and galleries in Italy; Lucca is a wonderfully gracious and civilised little town, and nearby Pisa has its famous tower and cathedral. Cortona and Montepulciano are charming towns, full of medieval corners, with views across sublime Tuscan countryside. Among the villages, San Gimignano stands out, thanks to its beautiful tower-filled medieval skyline.

'A place overflowing with everything that makes for ease, for plenty, for beauty, for interest and good example'

HENRY JAMES
Italian Hours (1909)

What to See in Tuscany

AREZZO ✪

This largely modern town merits a visit if only for Piero della Francesca's *The Legend of the True Cross* (1452–66), one of Italy's most famous fresco cycles. Ranged across the chancel of **San Francesco**, a church at the heart of the old town, the cycle describes how the tree from which Eve plucked the forbidden fruit becomes the cross of Christ's crucifixion. Although damaged in places, the frescoes are being restored, emphasising the calm colouring and subtlety for which Piero is renowned.

Make sure you also visit the Piazza Grande, the town's precipitously sloping main square, which is graced by the Loggia di Vasari (1573) and Palazzetto della Fraternità della Laici, built for a lay confraternity, and distinguished by a beautiful doorway and lunette tabernacle (1434) by Bernardino Rossellino. To its left protrudes the arcaded apse of Santa Maria, a lovely Romanesque church whose façade looks over the nearby Corso Italia. The interior has a superb altarpiece (1320) by Pietro Lorenzetti.

To the north stands the **Duomo**, whose airy Gothic interior is known for Piero della Francesca's fresco of *Mary Magdalene* and 14th-century *Tomb of Bishop Guido Tarlati* (end of the north aisle). Also worth a look are the cathedral museum, filled with paintings, sculpture and terracotta, the nearby **Casa Vasari**, birthplace of the 16th-century painter and writer and the **Museo d'Arte Medievale e Moderna**, with an eclectic assortment of paintings and artefacts, including five rooms of ceramics and paintings by the *Macchiaioli*, the so-called 'Italian Impressionists'.

✚ 65E4
San Francesco
✉ Piazza San Francesco
☎ 0575/20 630
🕐 Daily 8:30–12, 2–6:30
♿ Good
🎫 Free

Duomo
✉ Piazza del Duomo
☎ 0575/23 991
🕐 Daily 8:30–12:30, 3–6:30
♿ Few
🎫 Free

Casa Vasari
✉ Via XX Settembre 55
☎ 0575/300 301
🕐 Tue–Sat 9–7, Sun 9–1:30
♿ Few
🎫 Free

Museo d'Arte Medievale e Moderna
✉ Via di San Lorentino 8
☎ 0575/300 301
🕐 Tue–Sat 9–7, Sun 9–1:30.
   Closed Mon and 1 Jan, 1
   May, 25 Dec
♿ Few
🎫 Expensive

ℹ Tourist office: Piazza della
   Repubblica 22
   (☎ 0575/377 678)

The Piazza Grande, with Santa Maria's arcaded apse and Rossellino's beautiful Renaissance doorway

CORTONA ⭐⭐

Etruscan Cortona is a beguiling little hill town, with ancient walls ringed with olives and vineyards and twisting cobbled lanes and belvederes giving sweeping views over the surrounding countryside. A short walk from Piazza della Repubblica, which forms the old centre, leads to the **Museo Diocesano**, a museum noted for its handful of marvellous Renaissance paintings. The best-known are the glorious *Annunciation* (1428–30) and *Madonna Enthroned with Saints*, both by Fra Angelico, together with works by Pietro Lorenzetti, Sassetta, Bartolomeo della Gatta and the local-born Luca Signorelli.

The town's other major gallery is the excellent **Museo dell'Accademia Etrusca**, packed with a wide-ranging collection of Etruscan artefacts, Renaissance ivories, porcelain, ceramics, miniatures, coins and jewellery. Its highlights are an unusual 5th-century BC Etruscan 'chandelier' and a reconstructed Etruscan tomb, (on the upper floor.)

You should also visit San Niccolò, a church approached through a charming little walled garden and dominated by an intriguing double-sided altarpiece by Luca Signorelli. San Domenico has another work by Signorelli, a *Madonna and Saints*, while San Francesco boasts a fine *Annunciation* by Pietro da Cortona, another local painter. Some way outside the walls stands Santa Maria del Calcinaio, a distinguished but rather austere Renaissance church. A far better destination if you want to stretch your legs is the Fortezza Medicea, a ruined Medici fortress at the top of the town, which offers sensational views across Lake Trasimeno and the Umbrian hills.

➕ 65E3

Museo Diocesano
✉ Piazza del Duomo 1
☎ 0575/62 830
🕐 May–Sep, Tue–Sun 9–1, 3–6:30; Oct–May, Tue–Sun 9–1, 3–5
♿ Few
💷 Moderate

Museo dell'Accademia Etrusca
✉ Palazzo Casali, Piazza Signorelli 19
☎ 0575/630 415 or 637 235
🕐 May–Sep, Tue–Sun 10–1, 4–7; Oct–Apr, Tue–Sun 9–1, 3–5
♿ Few
💷 Moderate

ℹ Tourist office: Via Nazionale 42 (☎ 0575/630 352)

A view over the medieval rooftops of Cortona

Lucca

Lucca is one of Tuscany's gems, an immediately likeable place of cobbled streets, tiny Romanesque churches, bristling towers and lovely medieval buildings: the sort of place, in the words of Henry James, 'overflowing with everything that makes for ease, for plenty, for beauty, for interest and good example' (*Italian Hours*, 1909). The town began life as a Roman colony, later becoming Tuscany's first Christian town and the seat of the region's Imperial rulers (the Margraves). Its medieval wealth was second only to Florence, thanks to its banking and textiles, allowing it to dominate western Tuscany for centuries. Independent until 1799, it passed to Napoleon in 1809 (the town was ruled by his sister, Elisa Baciocchi), and then to the Grand Duchy of Tuscany in 1847.

The bell-tower of Lucca's ancient cathedral dates from 1070

ℹ️ Tourist office: Piazzale Giuseppe Verdi
(☎ 0583/419 689)

➕ 64B5

Giardino Botanico
✉️ Via dell'Orto Botanico 14
☎ 0583/442 160
🕐 May–Sep, Tue–Sun 9–12, 3:30–6:30; Oct–Apr, Tue–Sun 8–1. Closed Mon and 1 Jan, 1 May, 25 Dec
♿ Good 🖐 Moderate

Walking Lucca's streets is a pleasure in itself, but no trip to the city would be complete without wandering part of the city walls (4km in all), built in the 16th and 17th centuries as a defence against the Tuscan dukes. From their tree-lined ramparts you can enjoy panoramas over the pantiled rooftops, occasionally descending to explore sights such as the peaceful little **Giardino Botanico** (Botanic Gardens), in the city's southeast corner.

What to See in Lucca

DUOMO DI SAN MARTINO ✪✪✪

Lucca's cathedral is one of Tuscany's architectural master-pieces. The asymmetrical façade, begun in 1070, is famous for its carved reliefs, especially those over the central door – the *Life of St Martin* and *Labours of the Months* – and those of the left portal (1233), probably by Nicola Pisano. Matteo Civitali (1435–1501), local sculptor, took charge inside, where he was responsible for the inlaid pavement, pulpit, water stoups, two tombs in the south transept and the vast *Tempietto* (midway down the nave), built to house the *Volto Santo*, a 'true effigy' of Christ carved after the Crucifixion (probably a 13th-century fake). This statue, which is robed rather than naked, in the Byzantine style, is carried through the streets of Lucca on the eve of the Feast of the Holy Cross (13 September). The interior's highlight is Jacopo della Quercia's *Tomb of Illaria del Carretto* (1410), one of Italy's most beautiful tombs (it is currently housed off the right nave: there is a small admission charge to view it). The cathedral also contains paintings by Fra Bartolomeo, Bronzino, Tintoretto and Domenico Ghirlandaio. Near by the **Museo della Cattedrale** houses a collection of religious and other artefacts.

MUSEO NAZIONALE DI VILLA GUINIGI ✪✪

The Museo Nazionale di Villa Guinigi, at the eastern end of the town, has a major collection of sculpture, paintings and archaeological fragments, including artefacts dating back to the Etruscan and Roman periods. Among the exhibits are works by Jacopo della Quercia, Matteo Civitali, Fra Bartolomeo and paintings by anonymous Sienese and Lucchese masters. More paintings can be seen across the city in the **Pinacoteca Nazionale**, housed in the Palazzo Mansi, a wonderful rococo palace.

✚ 64B5

Museo della Cattedrale

✉ Via Arcivescovado

☎ 0583/490 530

🕐 May–Sep, Tue–Fri 10–6, Sat, Sun and public hols 10–7; Oct and Mar, Tue–Sun 10–6; Nov–Feb, Tue–Fri 10–4, Sat, Sun and public hols 10–5

♿ Few 🍽 Moderate

Museo Nazionale di Villa Guinigi

✉ Via della Quarquonia

☎ 0583/46 033

🕐 May–Sep: Tue–Sat 9–7, Sun and public hols 9–2, Oct–Apr: Tue–Sun 9–2. Closed Mon and 1 Jan, 1 May, 25 Dec

♿ Good 🍽 Moderate

✚ 64B5

Pinacoteca Nazionale

✉ Via Galli Tassi 43

☎ 0583/55 570

🕐 Tue–Sat 9–7, Sun and public hols 9–2. Closed Mon and 1 Jan, 1 May, 25 Dec

♿ Few

🍽 Expensive

🚩 64B5
✉ Piazza San Frediano
☎ None
🕐 Daily 9–12, 3:30–5
♿ Good: some steps
🎫 Free

Torre Guinigi

✉ Via Sant'Andrea 41
☎ 0583/48 524
🕐 Mar–Sep, daily 9–7:30;
Oct, daily 10–6; Nov–Feb,
daily 10–4:30. Closed 25
Dec
♿ Few
🎫 Moderate

*San Frediano's façade
mosaic depicts the
Ascension with the
Apostles below*

SAN FREDIANO ⭐⭐

San Frediano (1112–47), the third of Lucca's major
churches, is dominated by a superb 13th-century façade
mosaic, while the dark interior features a wealth of sculptures and paintings. Pride of place goes to the magnificent
Fonta Lustrale, a large and intricately carved 12th-century
font. Behind it, a carved *Annunciation* by Andrea della
Robbia, is framed by festoons of terracotta fruit. Close by is
the tomb of St Zita, patron saint of serving maids. The
Cappella Trenta (fourth chapel on the left) features two
pavement tombs and a sculpted altarpiece (1422) by Jacopo
della Quercia; the second chapel in the same aisle contains
the city's best fresco cycle: Amico Aspertini's 16th-century
scenes from the lives of San Frediano, St Augustine and the
Arrival of the Volto Santo in Lucca (see above). Just to the
southeast of the church is Piazza Anfiteatro, an evocative
square whose oval of crumbling houses mirrors the shape
of the Roman amphitheatre which stood here until the
12th century. Many were partly built with stone from the
amphitheatre.

A short distance south of Piazza Anfiteatro (walk via San
Pietro Somaldi for its lovely façade) brings you to the Torre
Guinigi, an eccentric city landmark built as a defensive
tower by the Guinigi, one of Lucca's leading medieval
families. A grove of ilex trees sprouts from its summit, and
it has lovely views over the city.

SAN MICHELE IN FORO ✪✪✪

Lucca's streets focus on Piazza San Michele, site of the old Roman forum (*foro*), and now home to San Michele, one of Italy's loveliest churches. Some 300 years in the making, its façade is a wonderful confection of pillars, arcades and tiny twisted columns. The interior, by contrast, is plain, apart from a della Robbia terracotta and Filippino Lippi's *Saints Jerome, Sebastian, Roch and Helena*. West of the square lies the **Casa Natale di Puccini**, birthplace of Giacomo Puccini (1858–1924), and now a museum of memorabilia. To the east, San Cristoforo's walls are engraved with the names of Lucca's war dead.

The pillars, arcades and tiny columns of San Michele in Foro

🚩 64B5

Casa Natale di Puccini

✉ Via di Poggio, Corte San Lorenzo 8

☎ 0583/584 028

🕐 May–Sep, Tue–Sun 10–1, 3–6; Oct–Apr, Tue–Sun 11–1, 3–5. Closed Mon and 1 Jan, 25 Dec

♿ Few

💵 Cheap

❓ Guided tours only

🔲 65D3

Fortezza
- ✉ Piazzale della Fortezza
- ☎ 0577/849 211
- 🕐 May–mid-Jul, Tue–Sun 9–1, 2:30–8; mid-Jul–mid-Sep, daily 9–1, 2:30–8; mid-Sep–Apr, Tue–Sun 9–1, 2–6
- 🍴 Wine and snacks from the *enoteca* (£)
- 🛈 Tourist office: Costa del Municipio 8, off Piazza del Popolo (☎ 0577/849 331)
- ♿ Few
- 💷 Castle and *enoteca*: free. Tower: moderate
- 🔲 Wine bar and shop on site

Museo Civico
- ✉ Via Ricasoli
- ☎ No tel
- 🕐 Ask at Tourist Office
- 🍴 Near by (£)
- ♿ Good
- 💷 Moderate

Sant'Antimo
- ✉ 1km from Castelnuovo dell'Abate
- ☎ 0577/835 659
- 🕐 Apr–Sep, daily 10:30–12:30, 3–6; Oct–Mar, daily 11–12.30, 3–5
- 🍴 Near by in Castelnuovo dell'Abate (£)
- ♿ Good
- 💷 Free

MONTALCINO ✪✪

Lofty Montalcino is one of Tuscany's most pleasing hilltowns, with picture-perfect streets, magnificent views and some of the best wine in Italy (many shops sell the ubiquitous *Brunello* and *Rosso di Montalcino*). A fairy-tale **fortezza** (fortress) dominates the town's southern approaches, begun in 1361 and strengthened by Cosimo I in 1571 after the town had fallen to the Medici (Montalcino was the last town of the Sienese Republic to surrender to Florence). Inside is a little *enoteca* (wine bar) where you can sample local wines, along with a watch tower and battlements, with far-reaching views.

You can also buy wines at the Fiaschetteria Italiana, a pretty, turn-of-the-century café in Piazza del Popolo, the town's modest main square. On one side of the square stands the narrow Palazzo dei Priori (1292), on another the graceful arches of a Renaissance loggia. The town's new **Museo Civico** is housed in a monastery annexed to the fresco-filled church of Sant'Agostino. The museum is full of valuable wooden sculptures and wonderful Gothic and Renaissance paintings.

A few kilometres south of Montalcino lies **Sant'Antimo**, a superb Cistercian abbey beautifully situated in glorious pastoral countryside and reputedly founded by Charlemagne in 832, though most of the present Romanesque building dates from the 12th century. The stunning interior features several finely carved capitals: look for the second column on the right, where the capital shows *Daniel in the Lion's Den*. The ambulatory and its radiating chapels, unusual in Italian churches, were based on French models.

Montalcino's lovely Fiaschetteria Italiana is the perfect place to take time out from sightseeing

MONTEPULCIANO ✪✪

Ancient Montepulciano is the highest of the Tuscan hill-towns, gazing down from its wind-blown eyrie across Lake Trasimeno and Umbria's hazy hills. Strung along a narrow ridge, the town hinges around a single main street – the Corso – a precipitous climb which passes a succession of interesting churches and Renaissance palaces. Look out for the Palazzo Cocconi (No 70), attributed to Antonio Sangallo, Vignola's Palazzo Tarugi (No 82), and the unmistakable Palazzo Bucelli (No 73), whose lower walls are studded with ancient Etruscan funerary urns.

Further up the hill you pass Sant'Agostino, designed by Michelozzo, the Medici's favourite architect, and short detours take you to another pair of worthwhile churches: Santa Lucia and San Francesco. Pop in to the **Museo Civico**, home to a selection of Gothic and Renaissance works, and then recover your breath in the Piazza Grande, the town's main square. Here, the Palazzo Comunale's **tower** provides good views, while at Palazzo Cantucci, you can buy the town's famous red wine, *Vino Nobile di Montepulciano*.

Also here is the Duomo, whose high altar shelters Taddeo di Bartolo's radiant *Assumption* (1401), as well as fragments of Michelozzo's *Tomb of Bartolomeo Aragazzi* (1427–36). The baptistery chapel (first on the left) features a font and six bas-reliefs (1340) by Giovanni d'Agostino, as well as a della Robbia terracotta which frames a relief of the *Madonna and Child* attributed to Benedetto da Maiano.

Finally, leave time for the ten-minute walk southwest, beyond the town walls, to **San Biagio**, a celebrated Renaissance church (1518–45) designed by Antonio Sangallo the Elder. The intention was that the church should house a miracle-producing image of the Madonna.

✚ 65E3
ℹ Tourist office: Via Ricci 9
(☎ 0578/758 687 or
757 442)

Museo Civico
✉ Via Ricci 10
☎ 0578/716 935
🕐 Apr–Sep, Tue–Sun
10:30–12:30, also 4:30–7
in summer; in winter by
request through the
tourist office
🍴 Near by in Piazza
Grande (£)
♿ Few
💰 Moderate

Torre Comunale
✉ Palazzo Comunale, Piazza
Grande 1
☎ 0578/757 442 or 757 034
🕐 Mon–Sat 8–1
🍴 Near by in Piazza Grande
(£)
♿ None 💰 Free
❓ Ask attendant for access

San Biagio
✉ Via di San Biagio 14
☎ None
🕐 Daily 9–12, 3–6
🍴 Overlooking church (£)
♿ Good 💰 Free

Hilltop Montepulciano

75

Piazza Pio II, heart of Pienza, a 'planned' Renaissance village

PIENZA ✪✪

Pienza owes much of its present appearance to Aeneas Piccolomini, later Pope Pius II, who tried to turn the village – his birthplace – into a model Renaissance town. The transformation began in 1459, a year after he assumed the papacy, and was overseen by Bernardo Rossellino, one of the era's leading architects. In the event Pius died before his dream was realised, and only the cathedral, a papal lodging and handful of palaces were ever built.

Piazza Pio II forms the heart of the planned extravagance, dominated by the classically inspired façade of the **Duomo** (note Pius's garlanded coat of arms in the upper pediment). The lofty interior – now showing alarming signs of collapse – was inspired by German 'hall churches' Pius had seen on his travels around Europe. The tall windows – another papal whim – were designed to create a flood of light, symbolising the enlightenment of the age. Pius also commissioned the five beautiful Sienese altarpieces ranged around the walls.

To the Duomo's right stands the **Palazzo Piccolomini**, Pius's palace, distinguished by the glorious triple-tiered loggia and gardens to the rear. Like the town's walls and walkways, these provide some breathtaking views. Several rooms are open to the public, notably the papal bedroom and weapon-filled Sala d'Armi. To the left of the Duomo, the **Museo della Cattedrale** has a surprisingly good collection of tapestries, manuscripts, silverware and Sienese paintings. The highlight is a 14th-century papal cope. Be sure to visit the Pieve di Corsignano, an ancient parish church some five minutes' walk outside the village.

PISA

Pisa has far more to offer than its famous leaning tower (►25), not least the ensemble of sights on Piazza dei Miracoli, the broad grassy square which encloses not only the tower, but also the town's cathedral, Baptistery and Camposanto. Begun in 1152, the **Baptistery** (Italy's largest) is a mixture of Romanesque and Gothic, the latter added by Nicola and Giovanni Pisano between 1270 and 1290. Nicola also carved the exceptional pulpit (1260); the interior is otherwise bare, except for a fine octagonal font (1246) by Guido da Como.

The **cathedral** is earlier, dating from 1063, though most of the interior was remodelled after a disastrous fire in 1595. Among the survivors of the conflagration were the bronze doors (1180) and Giovanni Pisano's majestic pulpit. The piazza's third component, the marble-walled **Camposanto**, is a medieval cemetery whose once famous frescoes were all but obliterated by Allied bombing in 1944. Its tombs and fragments, however, are still worth a visit.

Bombing destroyed much else in Pisa, but spared the exhibits of the **Museo dell'Opera del Duomo**, a 23-room museum with an uneven collection of paintings, sculptures and other artefacts. The **Museo Nazionale di San Matteo**, Pisa's main civic museum, is similarly hit-and-miss, but includes works by Masaccio, Donatello and Simone Martini. The town's loveliest church is Santa Maria della Spina, named after a spine (*spina*) from Christ's Crown of Thorns kept inside.

64B5

Tourist office: Piazza della Stazione 11 and Piazza del Duomo (☎ 050/560 464, 542 291, 541 800 or 542 344)

Baptistery, Duomo, Camposanto and Museo dell'Opera del Duomo

Campo (Piazza) dei Miracoli

050/561 820 or 560 921

Apr–Sep, daily 8–8; Mar and Oct, daily 9–6; Nov–Feb, daily 9–5

Near by (£)

Duomo, Baptistery and Camposanto: good. Museo dell'Opera del Duomo: few

Duomo: free. Baptistery, Camposanto and Museo: moderate. Entrance also by combined ticket (expensive) with Museo delle Sinopie (museum of fresco 'cartoons')

Museo Nazionale di San Matteo

Lungarno Mediceo

050/541 865

Tue–Sat 9–7, Sun 9–1

Near by (£)

Good

Expensive

Exchanging views in front of Pisa's magnificent cathedral

64C5

Tourist office: Palazzo dei
Vescovi, Piazza del
Duomo 4 (☎ 0573/21
622)

**Battistero di San Giovanni
in Corte (Baptistery)**

Piazza del Duomo

0573/25 095

Apr–Sep, Tue–Sat 9–12,
4:30–6:30, Sun 9–12;
Oct–Mar, Tue–Sat 9–12,
5:30–6:30, Sun 9–12

Free

Museo Civico

Palazzo del Comune,
Piazza del Duomo

0573/371 296

Tue–Sat 9–1, 3–7 (earlier
in winter), Sun 9–12:30

Moderate

*Pistoia's historic centre is
filled with numerous
appealing monuments
such as this time-worn
Renaissance well*

PISTOIA

Pistoia's industrial outskirts deter most visitors, which is a
shame, for the town boasts a medieval centre and a group
of churches and monuments that stand comparison with
any in Tuscany. Piazza del Duomo, its captivating main
square, is home to the Campanile, a former Lombard
watch-tower; several medieval palaces; a 14th-century
Baptistery, and the arched façade of the town's cathedral.

The last contains a font by Benedetto da Maiano
(entrance wall) and the tomb of Cino da Pistoia (1337), writer
and friend of Dante. The chief highlight is the St James Altar
(1287–1456), Italy's finest piece of medieval silverware.
Weighing over a tonne, the work contains some 628 figures
and depicts episodes from the Old and New Testaments. To
the left and rear of the cathedral lies the **Museo Civico**, with
a collection of paintings and sculptures.

Elsewhere in the town be sure to see the 12th-century
church of San Bartolomeo in Pantano, which has a pulpit
(1250) by Guido da Como; San Giovanni Fuorcivitas, known
for its pulpit by Guglielmo da Pisa (1270), and Sant'Andrea,
also famous for its pulpit (1301), an outstanding work by
Giovanni Pisano. Sculpture of a different kind adorns the
façade of the Ospedale del Ceppo, a 13th-century hospital
decorated with a colourful glazed terracotta frieze
(1514–25) by Giovanni della Robbia (*The Seven Works of
Mercy*). Finally, visit the Cappella del Tau, a deconsecrated
church noted for its 14th-century Gothic frescoes.

Chianti Drive

Leave Siena (➤ 85–90) to the north, picking up the N222 towards Castellina in Chianti (21km). From Castellina take the N429 east to Radda in Chianti (10km). Two kilometres or so east of Radda at Villa there is an optional scenic circuit to the north (15km), via Volpaia. Return to the main road at Villa.

Distance
110km depending on optional detours

Time
Allow a day

Start/end point
Siena
✚ 65D3

Lunch
Restaurant (££)
✉ Badia di Coltibuono
☎ 0577/749031
🕓 Closed Mon

The N222 is one of the more scenic roads in Chianti, but like many in the region it is fairly twisting, so distances are often a good deal longer than they appear on the map. Both Castellina and Radda are major wine centres, and both have pretty centres, but their outskirts have been tarnished by new building. Volpaia has an evocative 16th-century castle and several watch-towers. If you can spare the time, this is worth the detour.

From Radda head east to Badia di Coltibuono (6km) and then drive south on the N408 to Gaiole in Chianti (5km). South of the village (3km), turn left and follow a lovely minor road past Castagnoli, Linari and San Gusmé (20km). Turn right on the N484 to Castello di Brolio (8km).

Badia is part of an abbey complex owned by one of Chianti's leading producers. You can eat in the restaurant here (see the panel opposite for details) or buy wine, honey and virgin olive oil from the estate shop. Gaiole is an unexceptional village, but the Castello di Brolio is more appealing: one of Chianti's oldest vineyards, it has been owned by the Ricasoli family since 1167. Wine can be bought here also, and there are occasional organised tours of the winery.

Chianti is best known for its famous red wines

From Brolio return to Siena (26km) on the N408 via San Giovanni.

San Gimignano

Tuscany's most famous village is a picture of medieval perfection, its famous towers rising above orange-tiled houses and atmospheric streets. Two superb churches, swathed with frescoes, add to its charm, only the summer crowds detracting from the village's appeal. An Etruscan and then a Roman settlement, it enjoyed its heyday during the Middle Ages, when its position, close to trade and pilgrimage routes, brought great prosperity. Family rivalries and the Black Death brought its eventual downfall, and in 1348 the village surrendered itself to the protection of Florence. Thereafter it became a sleepy backwater until the arrival of tourism this century.

San Gimignano's famous skyline has been likened to a 'medieval Manhattan'

➕ 64C4
🛈 Tourist Office: Piazza del Duomo 1
(☎ 0577/940 008)

A combined San Gimignano ticket gives admission to the Museo Civico, Torre Grossa, Cappella di Santa Fina (Collegiata), Museo d'Arte Sacra-Museo Etrusco and Museo Ornitologico (a museum of stuffed birds south of the Rocca).

What to See in San Gimignano

COLLEGIATA (▶ 18, TOP TEN)

MUSEO D'ARTE SACRA/MUSEO ETRUSCO ✪

An arch to the left of the Collegiata leads to San Gimignano's Baptistery, whose loggia is frescoed with an *Annunciation* (1482) by Ghirlandaio and Sebastiano Mainardi. The courtyard here contains the entrance to the Museo d'Arte Sacra and Museo Etrusco, modest museums with Etruscan remains, a *Madonna and Child* by Bartolo de Fredi, an early wooden Crucifix, exquisite illuminated choir books, and a marble bust of Onofrio di Pietro (1493), a local scholar, by Benedetto da Maiano.

➕ 64C4
✉ Piazza Pecori
☎ 0577/942 226
🕐 Apr–Sep, daily 9:30–7:30; Oct, Mar, Nov–Feb, Tue–Sun 9:30–12:30, 2:30–4:30
🍴 Near by (£) ♿ Few
💰 Expensive. Admission also by combined ticket

MUSEO CIVICO/TORRE GROSSA 😊😊😊

San Gimignano's principal museum is entered through a lovely courtyard, with a loggia partly covered in frescoes by Sodoma and Taddeo di Bartolo. After climbing the stairs you can either enter the museum or climb the Torre Grossa, the only village tower open to the public.

The museum's first room (downstairs) is the frescoed Sala di Dante, so-called because the poet spoke here in 1300 during a diplomatic mission from Florence. Its highlight is Lippo Memmi's eye-catching *Maestà* (1317). Stairs lead to the picture gallery, with a large salon and several smaller rooms on the right, one tiny stone-walled room to the left. Enter this first to see three quaint frescoes (1320) showing a husband and wife playing and taking a shared bath before climbing into bed.

In the other rooms are outstanding paintings by Filippino Lippi, Pintoricchio and Benozzo Gozzoli, and several vivid polyptychs describing the lives of saints Fina and San Gimignano (two of the village patron saints). Lookout, too, for a crucifixion by Coppo di Marcovaldo.

➕ 64C4
✉ Piazza del Duomo
☎ 0577/940 340
🕐 Mar–Oct, daily 9:30–7:30; Nov–Feb, Tue–Sun 9:30–1:30, 2:30–4:30
🍴 Near by (£)
♿ Few
🖐 Museum: moderate. Tower: moderate. Combined museum-tower ticket: expensive (see below)
❓ Combined museum-tower ticket available Apr–Sep 12:30–3, 6–7:30; Oct and Mar 12:30–2:30

81

Enjoy a drink in Piazza della Cisterna after exploring San Gimignano

---

✚ 64C4
ℹ Tourist office:
  Piazza del Duomo 1
  (☎ 0577/940 008)

Sant'Agostino
✉ Piazza Sant'Agostino
☎ None
🕐 Nov–Mar, daily
  7:30–noon, 3–6;
  May–Sep, daily
  7:30–noon, 3–7
🍴 Near by (£)
♿ Good: some steps
🎫 Free

PIAZZA DELLA CISTERNA

Most people approach San Gimignano's centre from Porta San Giovanni in the south. From here Via San Giovanni leads past San Francesco, a deconsecrated Pisan-Romanesque church which now serves as a *cantina* selling the village's celebrated white wine (▶ 42–3). Be sure to walk to the lovely little garden at the back for superb views. At the end of the street you enter Piazza della Cisterna, one of the village's two linked main squares (the other is Piazza del Duomo). The piazza takes its name from the public cistern (1273) which sits at its centre, though the square is more noteworthy for the various medieval palaces and towers on all sides.

ROCCA ✪

A short walk from Piazza del Duomo takes you to the Rocca, San Gimignano's old fortress, built in 1353 on the orders of the Florentines. Two centuries later another Florentine, Cosimo I, ordered its destruction (just one of the original towers survives). Today the ruins enclose a pleasant little park, with sweeping views from the old ramparts.

SANT'AGOSTINO ✪✪

The church of Sant'Agostino, begun in 1298, is best known for Benozzo Gozzoli's chancel frescoes of scenes from the *Life of St Augustine* (1463–7). The striking high altar painting, the *Coronation of the Virgin* (1483), is the work of Piero del Pollaiolo, while the frescoes on the *Life of the Virgin* (1356) on the walls of the chapel right of the high altar, are by Bartolo di Fredi. The latter are considered to be one of the Sienese painter's finest fresco cycles, the other being the Old Testament frescoes which can be seen in the Collegiata (▶ 18).

The rear wall contains the Cappella di San Bartolo (on the left as you enter), celebrated for its magnificent altar (1495) by Benedetto da Maiano. Its reliefs depict three miracles by San Bartolo, one of the village patron saints, who is buried in the chapel. The three figures above portray the Theological Virtues, while Sebastiano Mainardi's frescoes, to the left, show saints Lucy, Nicholas of Bari and Gimignano, the last holding the town of San Gimignano in his arms. The four half-figures (1318) on the church's left wall, by Mino da Fiesole, are believed to be part of Bartolo's original shrine. On the right (south) wall are several notable frescoes, including a *Madonna and Child with Eight Saints* (1494) by Pier Francesco Fiorentino and *Christ with the Symbols of the Passion* by Bartolo di Fredi.

Southern Tuscany Drive

Leave San Gimignano (➤ 80–2) and drive on minor roads southeast to Colle di Val d'Elsa (14km). Continue southeast to Monteriggioni (9km) before picking up the fast Rome–Florence superstrada. Follow this to Siena (➤ 85–90), then take the city's ring road south before picking up the N326 (22km) for Sinalunga.

Colle di Val d'Elsa is unattractive on its outskirts, but retains a beguiling medieval centre, with the Duomo, San Francesco and a clutch of smaller churches and museums all worth seeing. Unmissable Monteriggioni is a perfect village, consisting of a couple of streets and an unsullied set of old walls and towers.

Follow the N326 briefly before turning right (south) on the minor N438 to Asciano (20km). From Asciano take minor lanes south to Monte Oliveto Maggiore (9km), Then continue to Buonconvento (9km) and south to Montalcino (14km) and Sant'Antimo (10km, ➤ 74).

Distance
160km

Time
1–2 days depending on stops

Start point
San Gimignano
🔲 64C4

End point
Montepulciano
🔲 65E3

Lunch
Taverna Grappolo Blu (£–££)
📧 Via Sc ala di Moglio 1, off Via Mazzini
☎ 0577/847 150

Classic Tuscan countryside near San Quirico d'Orcia

The road to Asciano – a partly walled village with a trio of little museums – takes you through the *crete*, the Sienese 'badlands', a region of bare clay hills and distant views. The abbey of Monte Oliveto, an essential stop, is famous for its fresco cycles by Sodoma and Luca Signorelli.

From Sant'Antimo take minor roads east towards the main N2 (21km) past the village of Castiglione d'Orcia. Turn left on the N2 and detour briefly to Bagno Vignoni (2km), known for the old spa pool in its main square. Then visit the famous Romanesque Collegiata at San Quirico d'Orcia (6km) before picking up the N146 east to Pienza (10km, ➤ 76) and Montepulciano (13km, ➤ 75).

🛈 Tourist offices: Colle di Val d'Elsa Via Campana 18 (☎ 0577/920 015 summer only), Asciano Corso Matteotti (☎ 0577/719 510 or 718 745 summer only), San Quirico d'Orcia Via Dante Alighieri 33 (☎ 0577/897 211 summer only)

Siena

Siena is Italy's loveliest medieval city. Originally Etruscan, it became a Roman colony and later the capital of a medieval republic and the principal rival to Florence. Italy's finest piazza, the Campo, forms its heart, providing the stage for the Palio, a famous annual horse-race. Here, too, is the Palazzo Pubblico, home to some of the city's greatest works of art. Near by lie the treasure-filled Duomo, one of Italy's greatest Gothic buildings, and the Ospedale di Santa Maria della Scala, which houses two outstanding fresco cycles. Alongside the Duomo, the Museo dell'Opera shelters the most majestic of all Siena's paintings, Duccio's multi-panelled *Maestà*.

✚ 65D3
ℹ Tourist office: Piazza del Campo 56
(☎ 0577/280551)
◑ Summer, Mon–Sat 8:30–7:30; winter, Mon–Fri 8:30–6:30, Sat 8:30–1

What to See in Siena

Exhibits in the Museo dell'Opera del Duomo

CAMPO, PIAZZA DEL (▶ 16, TOP TEN)
DUOMO (▶ 20, TOP TEN)

MUSEO DELL'OPERA DEL DUOMO ✪✪✪

This museum of works removed from the Duomo for safe-keeping occupies part of a half-finished extension to the cathedral, which would have made it the largest church in Italy (work was abandoned following the Black Death in 1348). It opens with the Gallerie delle Statue, with a *tondo* by Donatello in the centre of the room, a *Madonna and Child* by Jacopo della Quercia (Siena's leading medieval sculptor), and a series of wall statues by Giovanni Pisano from the cathedral's façade. Upstairs, in a special room, stands Duccio's *Maestà* (1308–11), a magnificent work consisting of a vast main altarpiece and countless tiny panels. Other treats are the anonymous *Madonna dagli Occhi Grossi* (Madonna of the Large Eyes), and the view from the tower.

✚ 86B2
✉ Piazza de Duomo 8
☎ 0577/283 048
◑ Jan–mid-Mar and Nov–Dec, daily 9–1:30; mid-Mar–Sep, daily 9–7:30; Oct, daily 9–6
🍽 Near by (£)
♿ Good
Ⓜ Moderate

85

☩ 86B1
✉ Piazza del Duomo 2
☎ 0577/586 410
◷ Jan–Feb and Nov–Dec,
daily 10:30–1:30; Mar and
Oct, daily 10:30–4:30;
Apr–Sep, daily
10:30–5:30; May–Jun,
daily 10–6; Jul–Aug, daily
10–6:30
🍴 Shop and café (£)
♿ Very good
✋ Moderate

OSPEDALE DI SANTA MARIA DELLA SCALA ⊕⊕

For almost 800 years this large building opposite the Duomo served as an orphanage and hospital. Following its recent closure there are plans to turn it into a vast cultural centre. More and more of the medieval complex is being opened to the public, revealing superlative works of art hidden from view for centuries. Chief of these is a vast fresco cycle (1444) by Domenico di Bartolo and Vecchietta, whose perfectly preserved panels decorate what until recently was a large hospital ward. The pictures show the foundation and daily life of the medieval hospital. A smaller stone-vaulted chapel, the Sagrestia Vecchia, is decorated with another fresco cycle by Vecchietta, who sculpted the famous high altar statue of the *Risen Christ* in SS Annunziata, the hospital's former church. In the bowels of the building lies the eerie Oratorio di Santa Caterina della Notte, where St Catherine once passed nocturnal vigils.

Siena is full of atmospheric little side-streets

PALAZZO PUBBLICO ✪✪✪

The Palazzo Pubblico's medieval outline dominates the Campo's southern flank. Begun in 1297, it was designed as civic offices, and still houses various council departments. From its courtyard an entrance (on the left) leads to the **Torre del Mangia** (102m), reputedly named after its first bell-ringer, a wastrel whose nickname – the *Mangiaguadagni* – meant 'the eater of profits'. The views from the summit are breathtaking. A door to the right of the courtyard leads to the **Museo Civico**, a series of chambers decorated by Siena's leading medieval and Renaissance artists. Some of the city's most famous paintings are here, including Simone Martini's exquisite *Maestà* (1315–21) and the series of paintings by Ambrogio Lorenzetti on *Good and Bad Government* (1338). Look out for the equestrian portrait of *Guidoriccio da Fogliano*, opposite the *Maestà*, controversially attributed to Martini.

SIENA

➕ 87C2

Torre del Mangia
✉ Piazza del Campo 1
☎ 0577/292 263
🕐 Nov–Feb, daily 10–1; Mar, daily 10–4; Apr and Oct, daily 10–5; May–Jun, and Sep, daily 10–6; Jul–Aug, daily 10–7:30
🍴 Near by in Piazza del Campo (£–££)
♿ Few
🚌 Moderate
❓ The tower has 503 steps

Museo Civico
✉ Piazza del Campo 1
☎ 0577/292 263
🕐 Jan–Feb and Nov–Dec, Mon–Sat 9:30–1:30; Mar and Oct, Mon–Sat 9:30–6; Apr and Sep, Mon–Sat 9:30–6:30; May–Jun, Mon–Sat 9–7; Jul–Aug Mon–Sat 9–7:30, Sunday opening; May–Aug 9–1:30; Jan–Apr and Sep–Dec 9:30–1:30
🍴 Near by in Piazza del Campo (£–££)
♿ Good 🚌 Moderate

87C1
Palazzo Buonsignori, Via
San Pietro 29
0577/286 143 or 281 161
Summer, Tue–Sat 9–7,
Sun 8–1; winter, Tue–Sat
8:30–1.30, 2:30–4 or
5:30, Sun 8–6
Near by (£)
Good
Expensive

PINACOTECA NAZIONALE

Siena's Pinacoteca is one of Italy's finest art galleries, its warren of rooms tracing the development of Sienese painting over some 500 years. A lovely and distinct school, the Sienese painters – notably Duccio – drew their early inspiration from Byzantine art, revelling in gold backgrounds, sumptuous colouring and stylised Madonnas. Later artists – Pietro Lorenzetti and Simone Martini in particular – moulded these earlier styles to their own purpose, producing beautifully lyrical paintings whose influence was felt as far afield as England and the Netherlands. The gallery then deals with painters such as Sassetta and Giovanni di Paolo, who took stock of Florentine innovations, blending the traditional Sienese motifs with the new wave of Renaissance thinking. Finally the gallery touches on some of Siena's Mannerist stars.

87C1
Prato di Sant'Agostino
No tel
Irregular opening: consult
tourist office
Free

SANT'AGOSTINO

Begun in 1258, Sant'Agostino's interior was remodelled along baroque lines by Vanvitelli some 500 years later. The church keeps very irregular hours, but is well worth visiting for a handful of outstanding paintings. Perugino's *Crucifixion* (1506) occupies the second altar of the right (south) aisle. Alongside it, the Cappella Piccolomini contains an *Adoration of the Magi* (1518) by Sodoma and a 14th-century lunette fresco of the *Madonna and Child with Saints* by Ambrogio Lorenzetti. The Cappella Bichi in the south transept has more frescoes and two monochrome medallions by Luca Signorelli.

86B2
Piazza San Domenico
No tel
Daily 9–12, 3–5
Free

SAN DOMENICO

This vast Gothic church, begun by the Dominicans in 1226, is associated with St Catherine of Siena, Italy's joint patron saint (with St Francis). The Cappella delle Volte, right of the entrance, features a contemporary portrait (1414) of the saint, and the Cappella di Santa Caterina (midway down the right aisle) has frescoes of scenes from her life by Sodoma (1526). Her skull is kept in the chapel's altar taber-nacle. Left of the chapel is a detached fresco of the *Madonna and Child* by Pietro Lorenzetti, brother of Ambrogio (both probably died in the plague of 1384). The first chapel to the right of the high altar houses Matteo di Giovanni's triptych of the *Madonna and Child with Saints*. Adorning the high altar are a tabernacle and sculpted angels (1475) by Benedetto da Maiano, while the second chapel to its left has a *St Barbara and Saints* (Matteo di Giovanni's masterpiece) and *Madonna and Child* by Benvenuto di Giovanni.

Right: *Looking across the rooftops to San Domenico, a Gothic church begun in 1226*

SAN FRANCESCO ⭐

A fire in 1655 left San Francesco stripped of all but a few works of art. Surviving fragments include a *Crucifixion* (1331) by Pietro Lorenzetti (first chapel left of high altar) and two graphic frescoes by Pietro and his brother Ambrogio (third chapel). The sacristy has a fine polyptych by Lippo Vanni of the *Madonna and Child with Four Saints* (1370), and at the end of the right (south) aisle is the 14th-century tomb of the Tolomei. Outside the church is the **Oratorio di San Bernardino**, whose beautifully panelled upper chapel has 14 large frescoes by Sodoma, Beccafumi and Girolamo del Pacchia (1496–1518).

- 87D3
- ✉ Piazza San Francisco
- ☎ No tel
- 🕐 Church: daily 9–12, 3–5. Oratorio di San Bernardino: Apr–Nov, Mon–Sat 10:30–1:30, 3–5:30; Dec–Apr, Mon–Sat 10:30–1:30
- 🎫 Church: free. Oratorio: moderate
- 🍴 Near by (£) ♿ Few

SANTA MARIA DEI SERVI ⭐⭐

This outlying church is worth the walk for its works of art and the lovely view of the city from its shady terrace. The first main altar on the right contains the *Madonna di Bordone* (1261) by Coppo di Marcovaldo, a Florentine artist; the last altar on the right features Matteo di Giovanni's *Massacre of the Innocents* (1491). An earlier version of the latter subject by Pietro Lorenzetti occupies the right wall of the second chapel right of the high altar. Other works include *The Adoration of the Shepherds* (1404) by one of Lorenzetti's followers, Taddeo di Bartolo, *Madonna della Misericordia* (1431) by one of Taddeo's pupils, Giovanni di Paolo, and *Madonna del Belvedere* (1363) by Jacopo di Mino.

- 87D1
- ☎ No tel
- ✉ Piazza Manzoni
- 🕐 Daily 9–12:30, 3–5
- 🎫 Free

Did you know ?

Coppo di Marcovaldo was captured by the Sienese at the Battle of Montaperti in 1260 and forced to paint the Madonna in Santa Maria dei Servi as part of his ransom for release.

64C4

Museo d'Arte Sacra
✉ Via Roma 13
☎ 0588/86 290
🕐 Mid-Mar–mid-Oct, daily 9:30–1, 3–6:30; mid-Oct–mid-Mar, daily 9–1
💰 Expensive

Museo Etrusco Guarnacci
✉ Via Don Minzoni 15
☎ 0588/86 347
🕐 Apr–Sep, daily 9–1, 2:30–6; Oct–Mar, daily 10–2
💰 Expensive

Pinacoteca-Museo Civico
✉ Palazzo Minucci-Solaini, Via dei Sarti 1 (off Piazza dei Priori)
☎ 0588/87 580
🕐 Summer, daily 9:30–6; winter, daily 9–1, 3–6:30
💰 Expensive

❓ A single ticket *Biglietto Unico* is valid for the Museo Etrusco Guarnacci, Pinacoteca-Museo Civico and Teatro Romano-Archaeological Zone

ℹ Tourist Office: Piazza dei Priori 20 (☎ 0588/87 257 or 87 580)

VOLTERRA ⭐⭐

A windblown Etruscan town, Volterra commands wide views across eerie grey-brown hills, many riddled with the deposits of alum and alabaster that have long been the region's economic mainstay. Forbidding walls enclose the town's unspoilt heart, which focuses on the Piazza dei Priori, home to the Palazzo dei Priori (1208–57), known for Orcagna's painting of the *Annunciation* (1383) in the first-floor Sala del Consiglio. The square also contains the Torre del Porcellino (Piglet's Tower), named after the carved boar to the right of the top window. Here, too, is the former Bishops' Palace, part of which is taken up with the **Museo d'Arte Sacra**, three rooms of paintings and sculpture.

Backing on to the square is the Piazza del Duomo, site of a pretty Baptistery (currently closed for restoration) and the Duomo, celebrated for Mino da Fiesole's high altar tabernacle and sculpted angels (1471); an anonymous *Desposition* (chapel in the left transept); and a painted background by Benozzo Gozzoli, to two terracotta figures by Zaccaria da Voltera (north aisle). A little way north lies the **Pinacoteca-Museo Civico**, renowned for Rosso Fiorentino's *Descent from the Cross* (1521), a Mannerist masterpiece, and earlier Sienese and Florentine paintings Be sure to see the *balze*, Volterra's famous eroded cliffs; the Roman theatre and other sights in the town's Archaeolgocial Zone (to the north), and the wealth of Etruscan artefacts in the **Museo Etrusco Guarnacci**.

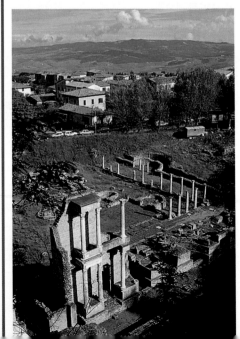

Volterra is well known for its range of Roman remains

Where To...

Florence

Prices

£ = under L35,000
££ = L35,000–L65,000
£££ = over L65,000

Meals

The Florentine breakfast (*prima colazione*) is usually a simple stand-up affair of *cappuccino* and plain, cream- or jam-filled croissants (*brioche or cornetti*). Unless breakfast is included in your room rate it is always better and cheaper to take it in a bar. Lunch (*pranzo*) starts around 12:30PM, but is rarely the extended blow-out of days gone by – this might be the time to save money by buying a picnic from a market or local food shop (*un alimentare*). Dinner (*cena*) is served from around 8PM.

Florence East

Alle Muratte (££)

Among the city's top-rated restaurants, and one of the first choices for a fairly-priced meal in surroundings which are welcoming and pleasant without being overly precious. The cooking is simple and assertive, revelling in innovative interpretations of traditional Tuscan and southern Italian dishes. There is also a little *Vineria* (wine bar) where you can enjoy a selection of dishes from the main menu at around half-price. Booking essential.

✉ **Via Ghibellina 52–54r** ☎ **055/240 618** 🕐 **Closed lunch, Mon & Aug** 🚌 **14, 23 & shuttle bus B**

Baraonda (££)

A gracious restaurant which has recently lost a little of its erstwhile popularity and culinary finesse, but still ranks among the city's better-known and most heavily frequented eating places. The cooking is straightforward Tuscan but with the odd twist.

✉ **Via Ghibellina 67r** ☎ **055/234 1171** 🕐 **Closed Mon lunch, Sun & Aug** 🚌 **14, shuttle bus B**

Caffè Concerto (££)

This restaurant lies well to the east of the city centre, close to the river, but the journey out here is worthwhile if you want an ambience which is a little exotic and out of the ordinary. The menu changes regularly, though the chefs' striving for innovation sometimes produces mixed results. In summer the terrace overlooking the Arno makes this a delightful place to enjoy a meal outdoors.

✉ **Lungarno Colombo 7** ☎ **055/677 377** 🕐 **Closed Sun, Jan & three weeks in Aug** 🚌 **23**

Cibreo (££–£££)

Most people rank this relaxed and well-known place just behind the Enoteca Pinchiorri in the roll-call of Florentine restaurants. Prices here, however, are much lower. It is a touchstone of simple Tuscan cooking, and has spawned a café and delicatessen, as well as a cheaper bistro-type annexe at the rear of the restaurant, where you can eat in cheaper, less relaxed surroundings.

✉ **Via del Verrocchio 8-Via dei Macci 118r** ☎ **055/234 1100** 🕐 **Closed Sun, Mon & Aug** 🚌 **6, 23**

Da Ganino (£–££)

Good places to eat close to the Duomo and central Via dei Calzaiuoli are surprisingly hard to find. This simple and reasonably priced restaurant is an exception to the rule, and is cheaper than the nearby Paoli (► below). It also has tables outside in a little square in the summer. If it is full try the adjacent Birreria Centrale, which also has outdoor tables.

✉ **Piazza dei Cimatori 4r** ☎ **055/214 125** 🕐 **Closed Sun** 🚌 **In the pedestrian zone: nearest services 1, 6, 7, 11, 14**

Dino (££)

Dino is one of the city's most venerable restaurants, and over the years has served consistently good Tuscan food to generations of Florentines. Suitable for family outings and business lunches alike.

✉ **Via Ghibellina 51r** ☎ **055/241 452** 🕐 **Closed Sun**

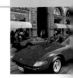

Enotecca Pinchiorri (£££)

There is no question that this is Florence's best (and most expensive) restaurant: many food writers place it among the best in Italy. Its lovely 15th-century setting, food and cellar (over 80,000 bottles from across the world) are without rival, though the rarified atmosphere and ceremony associated with eating here may not be to all tastes. An eight-course *degustazione* menu is available at L150,000. Jacket and tie recommended for men. Booking essential.

✉ **Via Ghibellina 87** ☎ **055/242 777** ⏲ **Closed Mon and Wed lunch, Sun & Aug** 🚌 **13, 23 & shuttle bus B**

Pallottino (£–££)

This is one of the city's newest restaurants, and in a short time has also become one of its busiest and trendiest. With luck it will survive (though prices may creep up), for the food suggests real skill in the kitchen. Service is of a high standard and the attention to detail impressive. Located just northwest of Piazza Santa Croce.

✉ **Via Isola delle Stinche 1r** ☎ **055/289 573** ⏲ **Closed Mon** 🚌 **13, 23 & shuttle bus B**

Paoli (££)

The food here may not be the best in the city, but few Florentine restaurants are as old or as beautiful. Most people come here for the atmospheric vaulted and frescoed dining room: the location is also very central (take the street off Via dei Calzaiuoli opposite Orsanmichele). Reserve a table or arrive early.

✉ **Via dei Tavolini 12r** ☎ **055/216 215** ⏲ **Closed Tue** 🚌 **In the pedestrian zone: nearest services 1, 6, 7, 11, 14**

Florence North

Antellesi (£–££)

This easy-going place is increasingly well known, though its popularity has pushed prices up and put pressure on the formerly relaxed service. Simple wooden tables and traditional Tuscan dishes such as *ribollita* and *bistecca*. Close to the Cappelle Medicee. Arrive early to be sure of a table. Note that there are a handful of tables at the front of the restaurant and far more tucked away to the rear.

✉ **Via Faenza 9r** ☎ **055/216 990** ⏲ **Daily** 🚌 **6, 11**

Don Chisciotte (££)

Smaller than many Florentine restaurants (just 40 covers) and with three high-vaulted and tastefully appointed dining rooms. Much – but not all – of Don Chisciotte's menu is devoted to fish, together with some interesting seafood and pasta combinations. Located in a street off the west side of Piazza dell'Indipendenza (northeast of the station).

✉ **Via Cosimo Ridolfi 4r** ☎ **055/475 430** ⏲ **Closed Sun, Mon lunch & Aug** 🚌 **All services to the railway station**

Le Fonticine (££)

This well-known and long-established family-run restaurant combines dishes from Tuscany and Emilia-Romagna. A rustic and self-conscious atmosphere suggest it has tourists in mind, but the food, especially the home-made pastas, is perfectly acceptable. Try the wild boar (*cinghiale*) and tripe (*trippa*) if you are feeling adventurous

✉ **Via Nazionale 79r** ☎ **055/282 106** ⏲ **Closed Sun eve, Mon & three weeks in Aug** 🚌 **All services to the railway station**

Menus

An Italian menu (*la lista*) begins with a list of starters (*antipasti*), followed by first courses (*primi or primi piatti*), the latter consisting of soups, pastas and risottos. The main course – meat or fish – is a *secondo*, with salad (*insalata*) and vegetables (*contorni*) served separately. Puddings (*dolci*), cheese (*formaggio*) and fruit (*frutta*) follow, often rounded off with coffee – Italians always have an *espresso, never* a cappuccino – liqueurs and *digestivi*. Bear in mind that few people wade through the entire menu, so in all but the smartest restaurants you can be happy with a pasta, salad and glass of wine. Italians often walk to a *gelateria* for an ice-cream as an alternative to a restaurant pudding. When ordering expensive meats, in particular the famous *bifstecca alla fiorentina*, the dish is often priced by the *etto* (100g): items thus priced are labelled *S.Q.* or *hg*.

Paying

The bill is *il conto* – at the end of the meal ask for *il conto, per favore* – and usually includes a cover charge per person known as *pane e coperto*, though this is increasingly frowned on and attempts are being made to make the charge illegal. Service (*servizio*) may also be added. Remember that bars and restaurants are required by law to give you a proper receipt (*una ricevuta*), so if you are unhappy with a semi-legible scrawl on a scrap of paper – still sometimes presented in cheaper places – you are within your rights to ask for a proper itemised bill.

Sabatini (£££)

This smart and historic restaurant was formerly one of Florence's most exalted dining places. The Italian-International food is now only intermittently outstanding, though still remains good enough to satisfy more than its fair share of Florentines. Service and the choice of wines are both generally excellent.

✉ Via Panzani 9a ☎ 055/282 802 🕐 Closed Mon 🚍 14, 17, 23

Taverna del Bronzino (££)

This rarefied but unstuffy restaurant has been an address of note for years, and a popular choice with business-people and smart Florentines. The cooking is traditional Tuscan, the service efficient and courteous. Pastas are good, especially the *linguine al pesto* and *cappellacci al cedro*. Both meat and fish dishes are available. To find the restaurant take Via San Gallo north from the Cenacolo di Sant'Apollonia: Via delle Ruote is the first left.

✉ Via delle Ruote 25r ☎ 055/495 220 🕐 Closed Sun & Aug 🚍 1, 6, 7, 11 & other services to San Marco

Florence West
Al Lume di Candela (££–£££)

Despite various changes of management, this restaurant has long remained true to its romantic name – 'By Candlelight'. Calm and elegant, it has a reputation for smoochy dining *à deux*, though the cooking, while good, is international rather than Tuscan in flavour. You also pay slightly over the odds for the ambience.

✉ Via delle Terme 23 ☎ 055/294 566 🕐 Closed lunch, Sun & Mon 🚍 6, 9, 11

Belle Donne (£–££)

This tiny place, full of convivial shared tables, is eye-catchingly festooned with mountainous displays of fruit, flowers and vegetables. Good, wholesome Tuscan cooking, with daily menus chalked on a blackboard. The informal ambience makes this a better bet for lunch or an early evening snack than for a full dinner. Located just southeast of Piazza Santa Maria Novella.

✉ Via delle Belle Donne 16r ☎ 238 2609 🕐 Closed Sat evening, Sun & Aug 🚍 6, 9, 11

Cantinetta Antinori (££)

Owned by one of Tuscany's oldest and most famous wine dynasties, this elegant wine bar uses wines, cheese and oils from the family's extensive estates. The beautiful panelled dining salons form part of an 18th-century *palazzo*, though the tables are close-packed and the service and ambience deliberately lively. A place for an up-market snack or light meal, but be sure to dress up.

✉ Piazza Antinori 3 ☎ 055/292 234 🕐 Closed Sat, Sun 🚍 6, 11, 31, 37

Coco Lezzone (££)

A well-known and rather trendy restaurant with simple, communal tables, where you mix with Florentines and fellow visitors. The white-tiled dining rooms date from the building's former role as a dairy. Cooking is rigorously Tuscan, though prices, while relatively reasonable, are a touch higher than the food deserves: you are paying here for atmosphere and 'authenticity'. You may also be expected to move on to make way for new diners.

✉ **Via del Parioncino 26, off Lungarno Corsini** ☎ **055/287 178** 🕒 **Closed Sun, last week of Jul & all of Aug** 🚌 **11, 31, 32, 36, 37**

Latini (£)
A cheap, cheerful and much-frequented *trattoria*, beloved of visitors and Florentines alike, though the crowded tables and raucous atmosphere may not be to all tastes. Its popularity has recently seen a modest rise in prices and a slight fall in standards, though the robust Tuscan food remains as good as ever.

✉ **Via dei Palchetti, off Via della Vigna Nuova** ☎ **055/210 916** 🕒 **Closed Mon** 🚌 **11, 31, 32, 36, 37**

Oliviero (££)
A mixture of creative and conservative Florentine cooking which can range from the very good to the sublime: on its day this is one of the city's very best restaurants. This said, the service and kitchen output can sometimes be a little erratic.

✉ **Via delle Terme 51r** ☎ **055/287 643** 🕒 **Closed lunch, Sun & Aug** 🚌 **11, 31, 32, 36, 37**

Florence Oltrarno

Angiolino (£–££)
Food here can, on occasion, be slightly erratic, but this is a pretty and also reasonably priced restaurant that remains true to its Florentine culinary roots. The varied *antipasti* are particularly good.

✉ **Via Santo Spirito 36r** ☎ **055/239 8976** 🕒 **Closed Sun evening, Mon & late Jul–mid-Aug** 🚌 **Shuttle bus B**

Cammillo (££–£££)
A boisterous, family-run place of long-standing appeal to foreign (especially US) visitors. Do not be fooled by the *faux* rustic décor, for when the bill comes it is likely to be similar to that in other more 'up-market' restaurants. Prices and bustle apart, the food is usually good, in particular the celebrated *fritto misto*.

✉ **Borgo San Jacopo 57r** ☎ **055/212 427** 🕒 **Wed, Thu & three weeks in Aug** 🚌 **Shuttle bus B**

Il Cantinone del Gallo Nero (£)
A glorified wine bar housed in fine vaulted cellar, with a wide variety of starters and hot and cold snacks. Food can be accompanied by wines from the Gallo Nero (Black Cockerel) regional consortium of Chianti producers.

✉ **Via Santo Spirito 6r** ☎ **055/218 898** 🕒 **Closed Sun & Aug** 🚌 **Shuttle bus B**

Casalinga (£)
Sit down with local workers and artisans to tuck in to classic Florentine fare at this cheap and authentic *trattoria*, one of a dying breed in Florence and many other Italian cities. Located in the street leading east from Piazza Santo Spirito.

✉ **Via dei Michelozzi 9r** ☎ **055/218 624** 🕒 **Sun & three weeks in Aug** 🚌 **Shuttle bus B**

Le Quattro Stagione (££–£££)
You are on safe ground here if you are content with good, basic Florentine food made with fresh ingredients and a homely approach. Try the roast lamb stuffed with artichokes.

✉ **Via Maggio 61r** ☎ **055/218 906** 🕒 **Closed Sun, Aug & 1 week at Christmas** 🚌 **Shuttle bus B**

Water
Tuscan and Florentine water in hotels and elsewhere is perfectly safe to drink. Water from drinking fountains in towns is also safe, unless labelled *acqua non potabile*. Bottled water, if you prefer it, is widely available, and is invariably ordered with a meal. You may have it fizzy (*acqua gassata* or *con gas*) or still (*acqua naturale*, *liscia* or *non gassata*). Ask for a full bottle (*un litro*), a half bottle (*mezzo litro* or *mezza bottiglia*) or a glass (*un bicchiere*).

Tuscany

Wine and Beer

House wine is *vino della casa*, and in cheaper *trattorie* is sometimes available in half- or quarter litre jugs – ask for *un quarto* or *mezzo litro di vino*. Most beer (*birra*) in Italy is of the yellow, lager-type variety, though darker British-type ale (*birra scura*) is becoming increasingly popular. The cheapest and most usual way to buy beer is from the keg (*una birra alla spina*) – bottled beers, especially foreign ones, are more expensive. The best Italian brands are Peroni, Dreher and Nastro Azzurro. As for size, ask for small (*una birra piccola*) – 25cl or 33cl; a *media* (50cl) or a *grande* (litre).

Arezzo

Antica Osteria L'Agania (£)

An authentic and intimate Tuscan *trattoria* (just 40 covers), with a good choice of local dishes based on the region's traditional cooking: things like *polenta*, *panzanella* (Tuscan salad), *minestrone*, *ribollita* and *coniglio alla porchetta*. Located just south of Piazza Grande.

✉ **Via Mazzini 10** ☎ **0575/25 381** 🕐 **Closed Mon**

Buca di San Francesco (£–££)

This is the best-known of Arezzo's restaurants among visitors, largely because it stands close to San Francesco and Piero della Francesca's frescoes. The ambience is a little austere, the food reasonable but not exceptional and the prices a touch over the odds.

✉ **Via San Francesco 1** ☎ **0575/23 271** 🕐 **Closed Mon evening, Tue & Jul**

La Lancia d'Oro (££)

First choice for a treat, if only for the Piazza Grande setting. Well-executed local specialities such as filling *zuppa di farro* and a variety of tender grilled meats. Fresh fish is sometimes available on Fridays.

✉ **Piazza Grande 18, Logge Vasari** ☎ **0575/21 033** 🕐 **Closed Mon**

Il Saraceno (£)

A stone's throw from L'Agania and offering a similarly authentic *trattoria* experience (though with three times as many covers). The food is perhaps a touch better, with superb desserts (try the *marscarpone al caffè*), mouthwatering

ribollita, succulent *zuppa di porcini* and decadent *ravioli al tartufo*.

✉ **Via Mazzini 6B** ☎ **0575/27 644** 🕐 **Closed Wed & Jul**

Castellina in Chianti

L'Albergaccio (££)

Any tour of Chianti will probably require a stop for lunch: Castellina has two good options. This is marginally the better and more expensive of the two. The dining room is pretty and in good weather you can eat outdoors. The food is classic Tuscan, with the bonus of home-made pastas,

✉ **Via Fiorentina 35** ☎ **0577/741 042** 🕐 **Closed Sun & between Jan & Feb**

Antica Trattoria La Torre (££)

This is fine *trattoria* of the old school, with a traditional look and reliable, steadfast service. Sundays can be busy, with service slow as a result, so go prepared for a leisurely lunch.

✉ **Piazza del Comune** ☎ **0577/740 236** 🕐 **Closed Fri & two weeks in Sep**

Colle di Val d'Elsa

L'Antica Trattoria (£££)

Despite its less than perfect position – in the lower and newer part of Colle on a square bustling with cars and buses – the chances are you will have one of your better Tuscan meals in this superb Michelin-starred restaurant. As well as much-loved staples such as *zuppa di legumi* and *l'anatra all uva* (duck with grapes) patron Enrico Paradisi regularly experiments with new and invariably successful dishes.

✉ **Piazza Arnolfo 32**

☎ 0577/923 747 🕐 Closed
Tue, Wed lunch Nov–Mar, Sat
lunch Jun–Oct, two weeks in
Aug

Cortona
La Loggetta (££)
Located at the heart of
Cortona on a loggia
overlooking Piazza della
Repubblica, one of the
town's main squares. A calm
medieval interior, complete
with brick vaulting, and
assured traditional Italian
cooking.
✉ Piazza Pescheria 3 ☎
0575/630 575 🕐 Closed Mon

Il Preludo (£–££)
Housed in part of a medieval
palazzo at the heart of
Cortona, this pleasant
restaurant offers food in a
classic Tuscan mould,
enlivened with occasional
touches of invention. Pastas
and *antipasti* are all home-
made, the *risotti*, in
particular, being especially
good.
✉ Via Guelfa 11 ☎ 0575/630
104 🕐 Closed Mon

Lucca
Antico Caffè delle Mura
(££)
In business over a century,
this refined and atmospheric
restaurant is housed in a fine
neo-classical building on a
bastion of Lucca's 16th-
century walls (on the city's
southern edge). The food is
reasonable and the
surroundings evocative.
✉ Piazzale Vittorio Emanuele
II ☎ 0583/47 962 🕐 Closed
Tue

La Buca di Sant'Antonio
(££)
Standards are not quite what
they were at Lucca's premier
restaurant (it has had a
Michelin star in the past), but
the traditional cooking,
central location and pleasant
atmosphere still make a
winning combination. Dishes

perfected over 40 years
include *bacalà*, delicate
ravioli di ricotta, and *risotto*.
✉ Via della Cervia 1–3
☎ 0583/55 881 🕐 Closed
Sun evening, Mon, last three
weeks of Jan & last three
weeks of Aug

Da Leo Fratelli Buralli (£)
A busy, no-frills *trattoria*
aimed at providing ravenous
Lucchese workers with a
reasonably priced lunch. Its
city centre location,
however – just off Piazza
San Michele – also makes it
a good evening option. The
cooking has predictable
Tuscan-Lucchese leanings.
✉ Via Tegrini 1 ☎ 0583/492
236 🕐 Closed Sun evening

Puccini (££–£££)
A lovely city centre
restaurant, located stone's
throw from the birthplace of
Puccini. Fish and seafood
are the menu's sole staples
– hence the high prices –
with the various *ravioli* a
delicious first course choice.
✉ Corte San Lorenzo 1–2 ☎
0583/316 116 🕐 Closed Wed
lunch, Tue

Montalcino
Cucina di Edgardo (££)
Eating in Montalcino's
highest reputed restaurant is
something of a risk, for
while the food can be good
– and the setting pleasing –
the occasionally far-fetched
leanings towards *nouvelle
cuisine* are not always a
success.
✉ Via Soccorso Saloni 21
☎ 0577/848 232 🕐 Closed
Wed

Il Moro (£)
The first choice for a
straightforward meal in
modern *trattoria* surroundings at prices that will not
break the bank.
✉ Via Mazzini 44
☎ 0577/849 384 🕐 Closed
Thu

After Dinner
The classic after-dinner
drink in Tuscany is Vin
Santo, or holy wine, an
amber-coloured dessert
wine often drunk with
small almond biscuits
(*cantucci* or *cantuccini*).
The aniseed-flavoured
Sambuca and almond-
based Amaretto are also
well-known, though
Italians tend to favour
amaro (literally 'bitter'), an
almost medicinal tipple of
herbs, wines and secret
ingredients. The best
brands are Averna,
Ramazotti and the
extremely bitter Fernet-
Branca. The best Italian
brandy is Vecchia
Romagna.

Soft Drinks
Italian bars have a wonderful selection of bottled fruit drinks (*un succo di frutta*) available in flavours such as pear (*pera*), apricot (*albicocca*) and peach (*peach*). Freshly squeezed orange juice is *una spremuta d'arancia*, freshly squeezed grapefruit *una spremuta di pompelmo*. Lemon Soda (the brand name) is a popular, refreshing and widely available bitter lemon drink. *Granita* is crushed ice covered in a syrup (usually coffee). A milk shake is *un frullato*, or a *frappé*, if made with ice-cream. *Crodini* is a popular but virulently coloured orange non-alcoholic aperitif. Ice is *ghiaccio*; a slice of lemon *uno spicchio di limone*.

Pizzeria San Giorgio (£)
The pizzas here are not the best in the world, but this is the most reasonably priced and easy-going of the town's many good eating places. Pastas and full meals also.

✉ **Via Soccorso Saloni** ☎ **None** 🕐 **Closed Mon**

Sciame (£–££)
An informal little bar with a top-rate *trattoria* to one side. Good for well-executed Tuscan basics with a twist.

✉ **Via Ricasoli 9** ☎ **0577/848 017** 🕐 **Closed Tue**

Taverna Grappola Blu (£–££)
Just two pleasant small stone-walled rooms and often superb and innovative food. Pastas are especially interesting and unusual. Increasingly popular, so be sure to book. Can be slow at busy times, however, and the piped classical music is unfortunate.

✉ **Via Scale di Moglio 1, signed off Via Mazzini** ☎ **0577/847 150** 🕐 **Closed Fri**

Montepulciano
Diva (£)
Diva is almost too good to be true: an old-world *trattoria* of a type virtually extinct in Tuscany. The menu is limited – little more than grilled meats for the main course – but all is perfectly cooked. It's popular and cheap, so be sure to arrive early to secure a table. If upstairs is full there is more room downstairs. Located in the lower part of town, just inside the walls.

✉ **Via Gracciano nel Corso 92** ☎ **0578/716 951** 🕐 **Closed Tue & three weeks in July**

Il Marzocco (£–££)
In a town not over-blessed with good restaurants this basic hotel restaurant makes a reliable standby if Diva is full or closed.

✉ **Piazza Savonarola 18** ☎ **0578/757 262** 🕐 **Closed Wed**

Monteriggioni
Il Pozzo (££)
This restaurant could hardly be in a more perfect gem of a village, and so starts with the advantages of a lovely setting. Its traditional but elevated food is worthy of the location, though some may find dishes such as quail, stuffed pigeon and wild boar in a heavy sauce a little too rich and robust. Simpler food is available at lower prices, though it is usually worth paying extra for the more inventive dishes.

✉ **Piazza Roma 2** ☎ **0577/304 127** 🕐 **Closed Mon, Sun evening, Jan (after Epiphany) & 1 week mid-Aug 15**

Pienza
Da Falco (£–££)
A welcoming, family-run *trattoria* just outside the walls, with several snug dining rooms and plenty of Tuscan specialities. Try the superb *gnocchi* or the *pecorino alla griglia* (sheep's cheese – a Pienzan delicacy – wrapped in ham and grilled).

✉ **Piazza Dante Alighieri 7** ☎ **0578/748 551** 🕐 **Closed Fri**

Latte di Luna (£–££)
Another friendly and traditional Pienzan restaurant located in an evocative little corner at the eastern end of Pienza's short main street. It is graced with a small terrace for *al fresco* eating in summer, together with an

ancient well incorporated into the medieval interior.

✉ **Via San Carlo 2–4**
☎ **0578/748 606** ⏰ **Closed Tue**

Pisa

La Mescita (£–££)
Much loved by locals and students from the nearby university faculties, this central little *trattoria* adds the occasional creative novelty to a menu dominated by a selection of Tuscan staples. Good selection of wines.

✉ **Via Cavalca 2** ☎ **050/544 294** ⏰ **Closed Sat lunch, Sun & Aug**

Numero Undici (£)
This is an off-shoot of the nearby *La Mescita*, offering a limited selection of hot dishes and puddings. Perhaps better for a snack and a glass of wine rather than a full meal. No credit cards

✉ **Via Cavalca 11** ☎ **050/544 294** ⏰ **Closed Sat lunch, Sun**

Osteria dei Cavalieri (£–££)
This has traditionally been one of the best-known and better regarded of Pisa's handful of central restaurants. Cooking is not especially distinguished, but the food is mostly reliable, fresh and well prepared. The choice of wines is good, and service generally jovial and accomplished. Located on the street running south from Piazza dei Cavalieri, Pisa's central main square.

✉ **Via San Frediano 16** ☎ **050/580 858** ⏰ **Closed Sat lunch, Sun**

Sergio (£££)
A serious and historic restaurant and the place to treat yourself if you are doing Pisa in style. Housed in a building begun in the 11th century, the locale has been an inn and a coffee-house in previous incarnations, and played host to all manner of illustrious names over the years. Elaborate cooking, professional service and stylish presentation.

✉ **Lungarno Pacinotti 1** ☎ **050/580** ⏰ **Closed Mon lunch, Sun & Jan**

Pistoia

Leon Rosso (£–££)
A pleasant and unassuming *trattoria* at the heart of Pistoia's medieval centre. The grilled meats are excellent – try the *coniglio al limone* (rabbit with lemon).

✉ **Via Panciatichi 4**
☎ **0573/29 230** ⏰ **Closed Sun & Aug**

San Gimignano

Osteria delle Catene (££)
One of San Gimignano's newer restaurants, but one which has already gained a good reputation. Prices may rise, but the cooking at present makes no down market compromises for the town's large number of tourists.

✉ **Via Mainardi 18**
☎ **0577/941 966** ⏰ **Closed Wed**

Ristorante Dorandò (£££)
The town's most expensive and most ambitious restaurant prides itself on creating 'historic' dishes of Renaissance and Etruscan vintage. This sounds dubious, but the results are usually excellent. The elegant ambience is offset by deliberately rustic touches.

Seasonal Food
The time of year you visit Tuscany will have a bearing on the food and specialities available. Fruit and vegetables are invariably home-grown in Italy, and exotic produce is rarely imported from abroad. January and February see the arrival of oranges from Sicily; asparagus and artichokes appear in early spring; late spring sees cherries in the shops, followed soon after by strawberries, apricots, peaches and plums. Autumn adds grapes and game to the Tuscan menu, notably wild boar (*cinghiale*), as well as seasonal specialities, such as truffles and wild mushrooms, especially the prized *porcini*, eaten grilled or added to pasta or risottos.

Bar Procedure

Tuscan bars may be either smart café-type places or functional refuges for a quick stand-up coffee. In all but the simplest village bars you usually pay a premium to sit down inside or outside, where waiter service is usually the norm. However, a single purchase allows you to sit and watch the world go by almost indefinitely. Standing up, the procedure is to pay for what you want first at the cash desk (*la cassa*) and take your receipt (*lo scontrino*) to the bar to order. In a busy bar a L200 lire 'tip' slapped down with your receipt often works wonders with the service.

✉ Vicolo dell'Oro 2, off Piazza della Cisterna ☎ 0577/941 862 🕓 Closed Mon & three weeks in Jan & Feb

Ristorante Il Pino (£–££)

The first choice restaurant (unless you wish to go up-market) in a town with a profusion of restaurants aimed largely at visitors. A pretty interior and plenty of tempting Tuscan tid-bits, especially among the mouthwatering *antipasti*.
✉ Via San Matteo 102 ☎ 0577/942 225 🕓 Closed Thu

Ristorante La Stella (£–££)

This pleasing but busy restaurant is often crammed with foreigners, thanks mainly to its reputation for good food at reasonable prices. Much of the produce comes from the owners' own farm.
✉ Via San Matteo 75 ☎ 0577/940 444 🕓 Closed Wed

Le Vecchie Mura (£)

Attractively set in a vaulted former stable, built within the old town walls. The atmosphere is friendly and the meals reasonable, and pizzas are also available in the evening. A good choice for an unpretentious and fairly priced meal.
✉ Via Piandornella 15 ☎ 0577/940 270 🕓 Closed Tue

Siena

Ai Marsili (££)

One of Siena's more serious and formal restaurants, and a good place to dress up and treat yourself. Service can be a little brusque, but the food is invariably good and the spacious dining room appealingly medieval.
✉ Via del Castro 3

☎ 0577/47 154 🕓 Closed Mon

Antica Osteria da Divo (£–££)

Some remarkable subterranean medieval dining rooms and an upstairs dining area which is almost as evocative: the food is also more than acceptable. Located a little way north of the Duomo.
✉ Via Franciosa 29 ☎ 0577/286 054 🕓 Closed Sun in winter

Le Campane (££)

Readers of Siena's local paper, *La Nazione*, recently voted this their favourite Sienese restaurant (and their second favourite overall across the province of Siena). A nice interior, with a few tables outside in summer, and a very central location.
✉ Via delle Campane 6 ☎ 0577/284 035 🕓 Closed Mon

Il Campo (£££)

Most of the restaurants on the Campo are either reasonable but forgettable pizzerias or over-priced tourist traps. However, it's not every day you have the chance to dine out in one of Europe's loveliest squares. So if you want to treat yourself, this is the restaurant to go for. Avoid the four tourist menus and go for the traditional *á la carte* options instead.
✉ Piazza del Campo 50 ☎ 0577/280 725 🕓 Closed Tue & four weeks in Jan & Feb

Da Enzo (££)

Currently one of the city's more popular restaurants. The tables are pressed close together, while the walls are decorated with the symbols of Siena's various *contrade*. The patron prides himself on his ingredients, many of which he produces himself. The daily set menu is good value.

✉ **Via Camollia 49**
☎ **0577/281 277** 🕐 **Closed Mon**

Garibaldi (£)

A cheap and reasonably cheerful *trattoria*, located beneath the small hotel of the same name.

✉ **Via Giovanni Dupré 18**
☎ **0577/284 204** 🕐 **Closed Sat**

Nello (££)

If Le Logge (almost opposite) is closed or full, or you wish to spend a little less, this easy-going restaurant makes an ideal alternative. You see the day's pasta being made and laid out as you enter – always a good sign – and the food when it arrives lives up to first impressions. A nice single medieval dining room, plus a few tables outside in summer.

✉ **Via del Porrione 28–30**
☎ **0577/289 043** 🕐 **Currently open daily, though may close Sun evening & Mon. Closed Feb**

Usteria del Fico Mezzo (£–££)

A tremendous addition to Siena's rather predictable crop of restaurants: innovative food, a tasteful single-room dining area (cool and pastel-painted); and good value, especially at lunchtime, when you can choose between a handful of set-price mini menus.

✉ **Via dei Termini 71** ☎ **0577/222 384** 🕐 **Closed Sun & mid-Jul to mid-Aug**

Osteria Le Logge (££)

This is Siena's prettiest restaurant, thanks to its lovely cabinet-lined interior – the building was formerly an old pharmacy. The food, however, once considered outstanding, has slipped recently. Located just a few steps east of the Campo. Be sure to book.

✉ **Via del Porrione 33**
☎ **0577/48 013** 🕐 **Closed Sun, part of Jun & Nov**

La Torre (££)

This rumbustuous single room *trattoria*, no longer the undiscovered gem it once was, plays slightly on its old-world authenticity, and prices have risen as a result. However, it remains popular, so arrive early or book in person to be sure of a table. Rarely any menu, so follow the advice of the waiter. The off-Campo location is convenient.

✉ **Via Salicotto 7**
☎ **0577/287 548** 🕐 **Closed Thu**

Volterra
Da Badò (£–££)

An excellent restaurant with a high reputation which is known for its well-cooked Volterran specialities.

✉ **Borgo San Lazzaro 9, just east of Volterra on the SS68 road**
☎ **0588/86 477** 🕐 **Closed Wed & Jul**

Trattoria del Sacco Fiorentino (£–££)

A newish restaurant which offers classic Tuscan cooking with a slight innovatory twist. Prices in the small adjoining *enoteca* (wine bar) area are lower.

✉ **Piazza XX Settembre 18**
☎ **0588/88 537** 🕐 **Closed Fri**

Tea

Tea with lemon (*un tè al limone*) is common in Italy. Tea with milk is not, so you have to ask for it specifically (*tè con latte*) and make sure the milk is cold (*con latte freddo*). Camomile (*camomilla*) is common after dinner in place of coffee, and iced tea (*tè freddo*) is widely available in summer.

Florence

Prices

£ = under L70,000–
L125,00 (double
room)

££ = L125,000–L175,000

£££ = over L175,000

Booking

Advance booking is always
a good idea in Florence
and Siena during busy
times of the year, though
both cities have hotel
agencies which will hunt
around for last-minute
rooms. In Florence the
agency (ITA) is on the
station concourse of the
Santa Maria Novella
railway station; in Siena it
is called Siena Hotels
Promotion and is found on
Viale Curatone, near the
bus terminal, opposite the
church of San Domenico.
If you are travelling around
Tuscany phone a couple of
days ahead to secure a
room, but note that the
idea of credit card advance
booking has not yet really
caught on in Italy.

Annalena (££)

An extremely popular three-
star pension-style hotel in
the Oltrarno. Housed in an
old Medici palace opposite
the Boboli gardens. Some of
the 20 rooms have terraces
and garden views.

✉ **Via Romana 34** ☎ **055/222
402; fax 055/222 403** 🚌 **11, 36**

Apollo (£)

One of the better hotels close
to the station and San Lorenzo
market area. Spacious rooms
with modern fittings. Walls
are covered in prints by the
owner, a noted photographer.

✉ **Via Faenza 77** ☎ **055/284
119; fax 055/210 101** 🚌 **All
services to Santa Maria Novella
railway station**

Beacci Tornabuoni (£££)

A venerable three-star hotel
converted from a 14th-
century palazzo on Florence's
premier shopping street. The
28 rooms are elegantly faded,
some smaller and less well
furnished than others. There
is a pleasant terrace.

✉ **Via dei Tornabuoni 3**
☎ **055/212 645 or 268 377; fax
055/283 594** 🚌 **6, 11, 36, 37**

Bretagna (£)

A charming and recently
upgraded pensione, some of
whose reasonably sized
rooms have views of the Arno.

✉ **Lungarno Corsini 6**
☎ **055/289 618; fax 055/289 619**
🚌 **Shuttle bus C**

Brunelleschi (£££)

A recent conversion based
around a fine medieval tower
in a quiet position just behind
Via dei Calzaiuoli. An
excellent and centrally
located four-star hotel, with
96 rooms.

✉ **Piazza Sant'Elisabetta 3**

☎ **055/562 068; fax 055/219 653**
🏠 **In the pedestrian zone:
closest services 1, 6, 7, 11, 14**

Excelsior (£££)

On balance the better of the
two famous and grand old
hotels on this rather
lacklustre square by the river.
The 160 rooms are nicely old-
world in look and feel, and
most have more character
than those of the *Grand*
opposite. Recently expanded
and renovated. Five-star.

✉ **Piazza Ognissanti 3**
☎ **055/264 201; fax 055/210 278**
🚌 **11, 17, shuttle bus C**

Helvetia & Bristol (£££)

Recent restoration has made
this Florence's finest luxury
(five-star) hotel. A central
position between Via dei
Tornabuoni and Piazza della
Repubblica makes it an ideal
base for shopping and
sightseeing.

✉ **Via dei Pescioni 2**
☎ **055/287 814; toll-free 1670
10058** 🚌 **6, 11, 36, 37**

Hermitage (££)

A very well-known three-star
hotel overlooking the Ponte
Vecchio; very popular with UK
and US visitors. Of the 29
rooms, those in the front are
double-glazed, those in the
back are quieter. Welcoming,
family-run atmosphere.

✉ **Vicolo Marzio 1, off Piazza
del Pesce** ☎ **055/287 216; fax
055/212 208** 🚌 **Shuttle bus B**

J & J (£££)

A quiet, small and intimate
four-star hotel in a former
16th-century monastery with
19 smart and very tasteful
rooms. Located slightly to
the east of the centre.
Popular with a select and
loyal group of clients, so be

certain to book well ahead.
✉ **Via di Mezzo** ☎ 055/234 5005; fax 055/240 282 🚌 shuttle bus B

Liana (£–££)

Housed in an 18th-century palace – the former home of the British Embassy – and decorated in places with frescoed ceilings and mosaic floors. Slightly spartan rooms (18), but fine communal parts and a shady little garden. Located well to the north-east of the centre, but within walking distance of Santa Croce and SS Annunziata. It has parking opportunities, so a good choice if you are travelling by car. Two-star.
✉ **Via V Alfieri 18** ☎ 055/245 303; fax 055/234 4596
🚌 **Shuttle bus C, 31, 32, 26**

Loggiato dei Serviti (££–£££)

An award-winning conversion in the vaulted interior of the Servites' former 16th-century confraternity building. Subtle, calm and airy rooms (29); advance booking essential. An excellent mid-priced choice (three-star).
✉ **Piazza Santissima Annunziata 3** ☎ 055/289 592 or 289 593; fax 055/219 165 🚌 **6, 31, 32**

Lungarno (££–£££)

A reasonably modern four-star Oltrarno hotel whose comfortable rooms (68) are divided between a new block (some with views of the river and Ponte Vecchio) and a converted 13th-century tower. The best rooms have terraces and views; all are decorated with antiques and a selection of the hotel's large collection of modern art.
✉ **Borgo San Jacopo 14** ☎ 055/264 2111; fax 055/268 437
🚌 **Shuttle bus B or C**

Morandi alla Crocetta (££–£££)

A small, and welcoming three-star hotel which forms part of a peaceful former 16th-century monastery just east of Piazza Santissima Annunziata. There are just ten rooms.
✉ **Via Laura 50** ☎ 055/234 4747; fax 055/248 0954 🚌 **1, 6, 7, 10, 11, 17**

Porta Rossa (££)

Housed in a 14th-century palace: one of the oldest hotels in Italy. Byron and Stendhal both stayed here. Three-star, 81 rooms.
✉ **Via Porta Rosa 19**
☎ 055/287 551; fax 055/282 179
🚌 **In the pedestrian zone: nearest services; 6,11,31,32,36,37**

Residenza (££)

Good value, given the excellent location, though rooms on the street can be noisy. Acceptable if rather unexciting rooms (24) ranged across the top floors of a 17th-century *palazzo*. Three-star.
✉ **Via dei Tornabuoni 8**
☎ 055/218 684; fax 055/284 197
🚌 **6, 11, 36, 37**

Scaletta (£–££)

Located on the top floor of a 15th century palace and usually remarkably peaceful given the Oltrarno location. Spacious and simply furnished rooms (13), together with two excellent terraces with views looking towards the Palazzo Pitti and Giardino di Boboli. Two-star.
✉ **Via Guicciardini 13**
☎ 055/283 028 or 214 255; fax 055/289 562 🚌 **11, 37 & shuttle buses B and C**

Sorelle Bandini (£)

Spacious rooms (13) of crumbling grandeur in a 16th-century palace of considerable Bohemian charm. Excellent value and often booked months ahead as a result. One-star.
✉ **Piazza Santo Spirito 9**
☎ 055/215 308; fax 055/282 761
🚌 **36, 37 & shuttle bus B**

Location

Where you stay in Florence is not of prime importance, most of the sights being within easy walking distance of the major hotels in all parts of the city centre. Cheaper hotels tend to be close to the station, which is less salubrious than elsewhere, without being too unpleasant. Also note the problems of noise (see panel ► 105) and be sure you are not in a peripheral hotel if taking a package or booking through an agency. In Tuscany many tour companies book hotels in Chianciano, an unlovely spa town with little to recommend it unless you are taking the waters. Even with a car it is inconvenient for most of the region's best sights.

Tuscany

Costs and Ratings
Italian hotels are rated
from one-star (basic) to
five-star (luxury), with the
price for each room within
a hotel being fixed by law
(it should be clearly
displayed on the room
door or close by).
However, prices for rooms
can vary within a hotel, so
if you are not happy with
your room ask to see
another. Hotels in lower
categories may also have
cheaper rooms with
private bathrooms. Look
out for hidden extras,
notably breakfast, which
may be included in the
room rate (check the back
of the door, where the
information should be
displayed with the room
price). Usually it is extra
and exorbitant, making it
better to take breakfast in
a bar if you have the
choice. Supplements may
also be levied for air-
conditioning.

Arezzo
Milano (££)
Located in a quiet side street
and a touch cheaper than its
nearby rival. The three-star
hotel was renovated in 1994,
so the simple, modern rooms
(27) appear bright and new.
✉ Via Madonna del Prato 83
☎ 0575/26 836; fax 0575/219 555

Cortona
Hotel San Luca (££)
A good three-star hotel;
many of the 56 rooms enjoy
fine views of the valley.
✉ Piazza Garibaldi 1
☎ 0575/630 460; fax 0575/630
105

Hotel San Michele (££)
A glorious Renaissance
palazzo whose elegance was
retained following its
conversion into a four-star,
40-room hotel. Plenty of old-
world splendour, and some
lantique-filled period rooms.
Central location.
✉ Via Guelfa 15 ☎ 0575/604
348; fax 0575/630 147

Lucca
Hotel Universo (££)
Lucca's best-known
traditional hotel. Many of the
60 comfortable old rooms
retaining an air of faded
grandeur: some have views
over the piazza. Three-star.
✉ Piazza del Giglio 1 ☎
0583/493 678; fax 0583/954 854

La Luna (£–££)
Centrally located close to the
evocative Piazza Anfiteatro.
The 30 rooms are a mixture
of old and new, some with
nice wooden ceilings and
pastel blue decoration. Three-
star.
✉ Corte Compagni 12, off Via
Fillungo ☎ 0583/493 634; fax
0583/490 021

Piccolo Hotel Puccini (£–££)
A splendid central position
close to Piazza San Michele.
Pleasant and well-presented
rooms (14), though the
communal parts are a little
cramped. Three-star.
✉ Via di Poggio 9 ☎ 0583/55
421; fax 0583/53 487

Montalcino
Dei Capitani (£–££)
An excellent central three-star
hotel which opened only in
1996. Rooms (29) to the rear,
plus the bar and terrace have
lovely views; a small
panoramic swimming pool
has been squeezed on to the
hillside on which the hotel is
built.
✉ Via Lapini 6, below Piazza
Cavour ☎ 0577/847 227; fax
0577/847 227

Il Giglio (£–££)m
An inn for over a century, this
moderately elegant three-star
hotel in the centre of town
has recently been improved
by renovation work. Many of
the 12 rooms enjoy views
over the *crete* and Orcia
valley.
✉ Via Soccorso Saloni 5 ☎
0577/848 167; fax 0577/848 167

Montepulciano
Duomo (£–££)
This is the best all-round mid-
priced hotel in town.
Located a few metres up the
street from the cathedral
square. Be sure to book
ahead.
✉ Via San Donato 14
☎ 0578/757 473; fax 0578/757 472

Pienza
Il Chiostro di Pienza Relais
(££–£££)
A new and beautifully
converted three-star hotel in
the centre of town; the 37

tasteful rooms form part of a former monastery and are entered from an elegant courtyard (*chiostro*).

✉ **Corso Il Rossellino 26**
☎ **0578/748 400; fax 0578/748 440**

Corsignano (££)

A modern and comfortable three-star hotel with slightly twee rooms (36), about 150m west of Piazza Dante and the town walls.

✉ **Via della Madonnina 11**
☎ **0578/748 501; fax 0578/748 166**

Pisa
Touring (££)

One of the best of a crop of impersonal hotels around the station. The 34 rooms are not terribly large, but all are modern if slightly functional.

✉ **Via Puccini 24 (off the northeast flank of Piazza della Stazione)** ☎ **050/46 374; fax 050/502 148**

Pistoia
Leon Bianco (££)

A central and reasonably peaceful position just south of Piazza del Duomo. Rooms on Via Cavour are perhaps less preferable than those away from the street. Three-star, 30 rooms.

✉ **Via Panciatichi 2**
☎ **0573/26 675; fax 0573/26 675**

San Gimignano
La Cisterna (££)

There is little to choose between San Gimignano's major central hotels: La Cisterna has 50 pleasing rooms and a perfect position at the heart of everything. Try for rooms with country or piazza views. Three-star.

✉ **Piazza della Cisterna 24**
☎ **0577/940 328; fax 0577/942 080**

Leon Bianco (££)

An elegant three-star hotel in a medieval town-house, a touch smaller and more

intimate than La Cisterna; 20 rooms.

✉ **Piazza della Cisterna 13**
☎ **0577/941 294; fax 0577/942 123**

Siena
Antica Torre (££)

Eight tasteful, mid-sized rooms in a converted medieval tower make this the most intimate and stylish mid-price option in the city. Booking essential.

✉ **Via Fiera Vecchia 7**
☎ **0577/222 255; fax 0577/222 255**

Duomo (££)

The 23 rooms are unexciting, though perfectly adequate, but the location is the best of the hotels in its price range. Three-star.

✉ **Via Stalloreggi 38**
☎ **0577/289 088; fax 0577/43 043**

Palazzo Ravizza (££–£££)

A peaceful three-star hotel in a peripheral but charming part of the city. A pension since 1929, it is housed in an 18th-century *palazzo*, 30 rooms of varying quality and charm. Booking essential. Undergoing extensive renovation at the time of writing.

✉ **Pian dei Mantellini 34**
☎ **0577/280 462; fax 0577/271 370**

Piccolo Hotel Etruria (£)

The nicest and thus most popular two-star hotel in the city, so the 13 rooms are quickly snapped up. Book as far ahead as possible.

✉ **Via delle Donzelle 3**
☎ **0577/288 088; fax 0577/288 461**

Tre Donzelle (£)

A good budget option close to the centre of town, but very well-known so advance booking is essential. One-star.

✉ **Via delle Donzelle 5**
☎ **0577/280 358**

Volterra
Etruria (£–££)

A reasonably priced three-star hotel on the main street in the centre of town.

✉ **Via Matteotti 32** ☎ **0588/87 377; fax 0588/87 377**

Noise

Noise of all descriptions is a fact of Italian life, whether you are in the countryside – bells and barking dogs – or the city (Vespas, cars, sirens, domestic discord, early-morning street cleaners, church bells and late-night revellers). Not even the most expensive hotels in Florence are immune to noise, though those with air-conditioning suffer fewer problems (hot summer nights mean you often have to have windows open). If you are a light sleeper, watch out for rooms on the street or busy piazza, and where possible ask for a back, garden or courtyard room. Better still, go armed with ear-plugs.

Florence

Tempting Toiletries
One of the world's oldest pharmacies, Officina di Santa Maria Novella has been in business since 1612, and still boasts frescoes, antique furniture and old-fashioned fittings. Many products are still made to recipes devised centuries ago by Dominican monks, and all rely only on natural ingredients and traditional production procedures. The soaps and creams are especially good and the pot-pourri is irresistible. This beautiful shop is located on Via della Scala 16 (☎ 055/216 276, 230 2437 or 288 658).

Books, Maps and Guides

Feltrinelli
An excellent central book shop with plenty of foreign titles, maps and guides.
✉ **Via Cavour 12** ☎ **055/292 196** 🚍 **6, 17, 23**

Libreria Le Monnier
For years this has been one of the best-stocked and most professional book shops in the city. Italian and international titles. Cultured and helpful staff.
✉ **Via San Gallo 53r, one block west of Via Cavour** ☎ **055/483 215 or 496 095** 🚍 **1, 6, 7**

Libreria Il Viaggio
A shop which specialises in travel guides to both Italy and abroad. It is also an agent for the Italian Touring Club (TCI), which produces definitive guides to Italy, and an approved seller of official state maps (useful for hiking).
✉ **Borgo degli Albizi 41r** ☎ **055/240 489** 🚍 **14, 23 & shuttle bus B**

Ceramics

Carnescchi
A large shop with a wide selection of ceramics from across Italy.
✉ **Via Guicciardini 4r** ☎ **055/239 8523** 🚍 **Shuttle buses B and C**

Sbigoli Terracotte
This family-run concern has been producing hand-made terracotta since 1850. Over the last 20 years it has also started making a wide variety of other ceramic ware.
✉ **Via Sant'Egidio 4r** ☎ **055/247 9713** 🚍 **14, 23**

Fashion

Emilio Pucci
The *doyen* of Florentine designers, Pucci has been creating beautiful clothes since the heady *dolce vita* days of the 1950s. The *haute couture* collection is shown in the Palazzo dei Pucci, the ready-to-wear range in the shops listed below.
✉ **Palazzo Pucci, Via de' Pucci 6** ☎ **055/283 061** 🚍 **1, 6, 7, 11, 17, 23**
✉ **Via della Vigna Nuova 97–99r** ☎ **294 028** 🚍 **In the pedestrian zone**
✉ **Via Ricasoli 36r** ☎ **055/287 622** 🚍 **In the pedestrian zone**

Marcella
Florentine women in the know come here for the sleekest lingerie, as well as a selection of the timeless clothes and accessories that have seen the shop prosper since its birth as a tiny boutique 30 years ago. An equally enticing men's shop has also opened.
Woman's Shop
✉ **Via dei Pecori 8r** ☎ **055/213 162** 🚍 **In the pedestrian zone**
Man's Shop
✉ **Marcella Uomo, Via Cerretani 7r** ☎ **055/216 352** 🚍 **In the pedestrian zone**

Marina
A shop for discerning women of all shapes, offering clothes from Max Mara, Marina Rinaldi and other designer names in all sizes, together with a good range of hats, shoes, bags and other accessories.
✉ **Via Martelli 29r** ☎ **055/284 097** 🚍 **In the pedestrian zone**

Max Mara
One of Italy's leading mid-range designer labels, with classic, simply cut clothes at affordable prices. Max & Co is a diffusion range aimed at a slightly younger market.
- ✉ Via dei Pecori 23r
- ☎ 055/287 761 🚌 In the pedestrian zone
- ✉ Max & Co, Via dei Calzaiuoli 89r ☎ 055/294 292
- 🚌 In the pedestrian zone

Principe
A range of designer and non-designer clothes at reasonable prices for men, women and children, all gathered under one roof.
- ✉ Via degli Strozzi 29r
- ☎ 055/292 764 🚌 In the pedestrian zone

Valentino
One of the great names of Italian fashion, whose clothes have been selling to the rich and famous for close on 40 years without ever losing their cachet.
- ✉ Via della Vigna Nuova 47r
- ☎ 055/293 142 or 293 143
- 🚌 In the pedestrian zone

Food and Wine

Cantinone del Gallo Nero
The Gallo Nero (Black Cockerel) is one of the most respected consortiums of loosely affiliated Chianti producers. This pretty cellar wine bar sells samples of their products.
- ✉ Via Santo Spirito 6r
- ☎ 055/218 898 🚌 Shuttle bus B

Pegna
Pegna has been in the business of selling mouth-watering food since 1860. The supermarket layout is a boon for those whose Italian may not be up to ordering in small delicatessens.
- ✉ Via dello studio 26r
- ☎ 055/282 701 🚌 In the pedestrian zone

Vera
One of the city's best delicatessens. The choice of cheese, in particular, is outstanding. Located just over the Ponte Santa Trínita.
- ✉ Piazza Frescobaldi 3r
- ☎ 055/215 465 🚌 Shuttle bus B

Jewellery

Bijoux Cascio
If you cannot afford the real thing come to this dazzling little shop, where the imitation jewellery is every bit as stylish and well-made.
- ✉ Via Por Santa Maria 1r
- ☎ 055/294 378 🚌 In pedestrian zone; Shuttle bus B or C

Caputi
One of the most famous names in top-class Italian costume jewellery.
- ✉ Borgo San Jacopo 78/82r
- ☎ 055/219 972 🚌 Shuttle bus B or C

Parenti
Florentines in search of the perfect gift often make a bee-line for this lovely and legendary shop. Silverware, porcelain, glass, ceramics, candles and jewellery.
- ✉ Via dei Tornabuoni 93r
- ☎ 055/214 438 🚌 6, 11

Torrini
Jacopo Torrini patented his mark in 1369. Six centuries later one of his descendants still runs one of the city's most distinguished jewellers.
- ✉ Piazza del Duomo 10r
- ☎ 055/230 2401 🚌 In the pedestrian zone

Vincenti
Of all the many old shops on the Ponte Vecchio, this jewellery shop is the only one to have been here since the 16th century.
- ✉ Ponte Vecchio 16r
- ☎ 055/287 241 or 291 065
- 🚌 In the pedestrian zone

Mercato Centrale
Florence's vast central market is an essential port of call, whether or not you intend to buy anything. Bursting with life and colour, its countless stalls sell a wide variety of fish, fruit, meat, bread and vegetables, together with all manner of delicacies such as hams, truffles, wild boar, cheese, honey, herbs, olive oil and plump porcini mushrooms. The market building, constructed in 1874, is one of Europe's oldest covered food halls, and was artfully extended in 1980 without destroying its wonderfully flamboyant atmosphere. Located at Piazza del Mercato Centrale; market days Mon–Fri 7–2, Sat 7–2, 4–8.

Supermarkets
The most prestigious department store in Florence is COIN, conveniently situated at the pedestrianised heart of the city in Via dei Calzaiuoli (☎ 280 531). It sells own-label and designer clothes, linens, kitchenware and a wide variety of general goods. UPIM is more down-market and forms part of a chain found all over Italy. It sells reasonably priced clothes and other goods from a large central store on the east side of Piazza della Repubblica (☎ 210 517).

Montalcino Wine Shops

Numerous shops around Montalcino sell the peerless Brunello di Montalcino, Tuscany's finest red wine, and the less-exalted but high quality Rosso di Montalcino. The following are the most pleasant or offer the best selections.

✉ Co-op, Via Ricasoli, near Sant'Agostino. The Co-op supermarket has a surprisingly good selection of local wines at very competitive prices.

✉ Fiaschetteria Italiana, Pizza del Popolo. A lovely 19th century café with a smart little *enoteca* to the rear.

✉ Fortezza, Pizzale-Fortezza. Montalcino's castle contains a busy and well-stocked wine shop.

✉ Enoteca Luciani-Grotta del Brunello, Via S Saloni. Has one of the town's bigger selections of wines, grappas and olive oil.

Leather Goods

Cellerini

Most Florentines wanting a bag make straight for this famous store. Some 600 different types of handbag and other luggage hang from the Renaissance ceiling of the 16th-century *palazzo* in which the shop is housed.

✉ Via del Sole 37r, off Via della Spada ☎ 055/282 533 🚌 6, 11 & shuttle bus C to Via dei Tornabuoni

Madova

This celebrated shop was founded in 1919 and sells a variety of beautiful gloves.

✉ Via Guicciardini 1r ☎ 055/239 6526 🚌 Shuttle buses B & C

Raspini

This designer name is a byword among Florentines for high-quality shoes, belts and other leather and fashion goods. There are several branches.

✉ Via Por Santa Maria 72r ☎ 055/215 796 🚌 In the pedestrian zone north of the Ponte Vecchio

Paper and Stationery

Il Papiro

Papiro is a chain of stationers selling marbled paper and marbled paper goods at keener prices than the city's more famous names.

✉ Via dei Tavolini 13r, off Via dei Calzaiuoli ☎ 055/213 823 🚌 In the pedestrian zone

✉ Via Cavour 55r ☎ 055/215 262 🚌 1, 6, 7

Parione

This shop has been open a mere 80 years, so it is not quite as famous or venerable as Pineider (see below). However, it is still a superb source of paper, pens, visiting cards, marbled paper and leather-bound books.

✉ Via del Parione 10r, off Piazza Santa Trínita ☎ 055/215 684 🚌 6 or 11 to Piazza Santa Trínita-Via dei Tornabuoni

Pineider

This celebrated stationery shop has been in Piazza della Signoria since 1774. Napoleon, Byron, Shelley, Puccini, Stendhal and Maria Callas are just a few of the famous who have corresponded on this paper. Elizabeth Taylor ordered visiting cards from the company to match her eyes.

✉ Piazza della Signoria 13r ☎ 055/284 655 🚌 In the pedestrian zone

✉ Via dei Tornabuoni 76r ☎ 055/211 605 🚌 6, 11 & shuttle bus C

Il Torchio

First-rate traditional Florentine marbled paper is available here either in sheets or as part of small paper-covered goods.

✉ Via dei Bardi 17 ☎ 055/234 2862 🚌 Shuttle buses B & C

Shoes

Beltrami

A well-known nationwide chain which sells not only shoes but a small selection of jackets.

✉ Via dei Tornabuoni 48r ☎ 055/287 779 🚌 6, 11, bus C

Fratelli Rossetti

Another country-wide chain for expensive high-quality shoes.

✉ Piazza della Repubblica 43–5r ☎ 055/216 656 🚌 In the pedestrian zone

Salvatore Ferragamo

This famous name has its origins in Florence. The city's flagship store contains a museum dedicated to the exquisite shoes made by the company over the years.

✉ Via dei Tornabuoni 16r ☎ 055/292 123 🚌 6, 11

Tuscany

Tuscany's smaller towns and villages – Siena excepted – are not great shopping centres. This said, many areas are known for a particular craft or food specialities.

Arts and Crafts

Most Tuscan towns have at least one shop selling ceramics and terracotta. The best choice, however, is found in more touristy towns such as Siena (► 86–91) and San Gimignano, though prices here are over rather the odds. With terracotta look out for factories on the outskirts of towns which sell directly to the public. Volterra is crammed with shops selling alabaster products, while Lucca, Pisa and the towns of the Versilia coast (Massa and Carrara) have many outlets selling the marble for which the region is famous. Linens and textiles are another good buy, with Lucca in particular having been renowned for centuries for its silk.

Food and Markets

Olive oil, one of Tuscany's most famous exports, need not be bought in fancy bottles at elevated prices. Perfectly good oils can be purchased from the region's many excellent CO-OP supermarkets. Pienza's sheep's cheese (*pecorino*) is highly regarded, as is the honey of Montalcino and Siena's spicy *panforte*. Every town has good food shops; most have a weekly market. The following are the best.

Lucca

This market in Via dei Bacchettoni, on the town's eastern fringes, is a general market of clothes, flowers, household goods. The Piazza del Carmine market is a covered food market.
- ✉ **Piazza del Bacchettoni**
- 🕐 **Daily**
- ✉ **Piazza del Carmine**
- 🕐 **Wed & Sat AM**

Montalcino

Old-fashioned market full of locals in the shadow of the town's fairytale fortress.
- ✉ **Piazzale Fortezza**
- 🕐 **Fri 7–1**

Montepulciano

A big bustling market by the old walls in the lower town.
- ✉ **Porta al Prato** 🕐 **Thu am**

Pienza

A tiny but interesting market just outside the old walls of the village.
- ✉ **Viale Mencatelli**
- 🕐 **Fri AM**

Pistoia
- ✉ **Piazza della Sala**
- 🕐 **Wed & Sat AM**

San Gimignano

An intimate little market in the village's main square.
- ✉ **Piazza del Duomo**
- 🕐 **Thu & Sat 7–1**

Siena

The general market in La Lizza is a huge affair. Piazza del Mercato is where many Sienese shop for everyday fruit and vegetables.
- ✉ **La Lizza, Viale Cesare Maccari**
- 🕐 **Wed AM** ✉ **Piazza del Mercato**
- 🕐 **Mon–Sat 7–1**

Volterra

A little market in one of the town's central main squares.
- ✉ **Piazza dei Priori** 🕐 **Sat 7:30–1:30**

Food Heaven

One of Tuscany's finest delicatessens, Maganelli, is found at the heart of Siena (Via di Città 73), its old-fashioned interior crammed with countless wines and brandies, 150 different grappas, 20 different balsamic vinegars, and shelf upon shelf of bottled jams, honeys, tomatoes, mushrooms, *pesto*, onions and other mouthwatering Tuscan specialities. It also has a good selection of Sienese delicacies such as *panforte* and *cantuccini*, the latter a special almond biscuit for dipping in dessert wines such as Vin Santo.

Florence

Italy and Children
Florence in summer can be a tough place for children, who can be forgiven for growing fractious in the heat and bored with the endless round of museums and historic buildings. At the same time, the Italians have a far more open-minded attitude to children than many (the smaller and blonder the better), and will usually make special provisions for them in hotels and restaurants. Children can ease the way in dealings with waiters, hotel staff and Italian officialdom in all its guises.

Food
Italian treats can save many a situation. Few children should be able to resist ice-cream, while a pizza by the slice (*pizza taglia*) from bakeries can also work wonders. Fresh-made milk-shakes (*frullati* or *frappé*) may also win children over, as may roast chestnuts from a streetside vendor in autumn or winter. The novelty of breakfast in a bar, or at an outside table, may also appeal.

Ice-cream

Carabe (£)
Come here for a *granita* (crushed ice with a choice of fruit syrup) or a tub of the excellent pistachio ice-cream.
✉ Via Ricasoli 60r ☎ 289 476

Häagen Daz (£)
A foreign name, but the ice-cream is good and the location central. Children may like a recognised brand.
✉ Piazza Signoria-Via Vacchereccia 3 ☎ 280 986

Granduca (£)
First stop for ice-cream on Florence's main Via dei Calzaiuoli.
✉ Via dei Calzaiuoli 57r
☎ No tel

Perché No!
A central *gelateria* which has been in business since 1939.
✉ Via dei Tavolini 19r ☎ 239 8969

Vivoli (£)
Vivoli is home to the very best ice-cream in Florence – perhaps even in Italy.
✉ Via Isole delle Stinche 7r
☎ 292 334

Galleries and Museums
There is no reason why children should not enjoy a small dose of carefully chosen culture. Michelangelo's *David*, which may be familiar from pictures, is a good place to start (► 19). The immediacy and detailed narrative of Gozzoli's frescoes in the Palazzo Medici-Riccardi may captivate, as may the comprehensible frescoes of Fra-Anglelico in San Marco (► 23). The suits of armour and Giambologna's sculptural menagerie in the Bargello should also be popular (► 22). Diverting museums include the Museo di Storia della Scienza (► 45) and Museo della Antica Casa Fiorentina (► 39).

Sights
The tremendous view from the Campanile should appeal to children (► 33), though you may well have trouble coaxing them up all the stairs (note that children may not enjoy the slightly claustrophobic passages of the cathedral dome). The Forte di Belvedere (see walk ► 41) is also attractive for similarly panoramic reasons, and has the added bonus that children can clamber around the walls and battlements, and let off steam.Children may also enjoy the sights and sounds, never mind the potential presents, of the Mercato Centrale and San Lorenzo street market. Be sure to hunt out the famous 'Porcellino', a much-loved bronze boar. The obvious novelty of the Ponte Vecchio should also appeal.

Tuscany

Outdoors

The Giardino di Boboli (► 38) is the most obvious place to let children off the leash in Florence. Further afield the chances for kids to run wild are more abundant. The novelty of lanscapes such as the *crete* south of Siena (► 92) may appeal more to older children, while the open spaces, wildlife and roam-at-will possibilties of the Alpi Apuane and Monte Amiata are also a possibility (► 12–13).

Beaches

The easiest beaches to reach from Florence are those of Viareggio, an elegant seaside resort about an hour from Florence on the train (regular seaside 'specials' run from the city in the summer). The sand is clean and the water safe, though many of the beaches are private – you pay a small fee to enjoy access to the sand, showers, bar and changing rooms. Further south, the (free) beach at Marina di Alberese (21km south-west of Grosseto) is among the best in Tuscany, but is only accessible by car.

Sights

The towers and streets of San Gimignano (► 80) should conjure up evocative medieval images for most children, as should the Campo and Torre della Mangia in Siena (► 85). Views from the tops of the towers in these towns and in Lucca (► 70) should also appeal, along with the old walls and fortresses of Montalcino (► 74), Monteriggioni (► 83) and Pienza (► 76). The Leaning Tower of Pisa, probably familiar to many children from pictures, will probably be as astonishing in real life for kids as it is for adults.

Galleries and Museums

As in Florence, older children should find many of Tuscany's museums and art galleries appealing in small doses. One of Tuscany's most popular Sunday excursions is to the Museo Leonardiano, a museum in the village of Vinci devoted to Leonardo da Vinci.

Museo Leonardiano

This interesting museum features beautiful models of Leonardo da Vinci's inventions drawn up from his notebooks, plus fascinating displays on the artist as inventor and engineer.
✉ Castello dei Conti Guidi, Vinci (11km north of Empoli)
☎ 0571/56 055 ◷ Daily, Mar–Oct 9:30–7, Nov–Feb 9:30–6
▥ Moderate

Parco di Pinocchio

One of the few sights specifically aimed at children is the Parco di Pinocchio. The storybook character was created by Carlo Lorenzini (1826–90), who took as his pen-name the name of the village (Collodi) where his mother was born. Located 15km east of Lucca, the park has pretty walkways through woods. There are mosaics depicting episodes from Pinocchio's 'life', various monsters, sharks and tableaux, and a toy shop
✉ Parco di Pinocchio, Collodi
☎ 0572/429 342 or 429 613
◷ Daily 8:30–dusk
▥ Moderate

Child Reductions

Children qualify for reductions on admittance charges in most Tuscan and Florentine museums and art galleries, though the idea of reduced price 'family' tickets has yet to catch on. Half-price tickets are also available for children under 12 on most buses and trains. Children under four travel free on trains. There are also reductions for families, worth considering if you intend to travel widely by train. Inquire about the Rail Europe Family Card (known as the *Carta Rail Europe F* in Italy) or Italy's own *Carta Famiglia* (available from main stations). The latter allows families of four travelling together to claim discounts of 30 per cent on the full fare. Few restaurants cater specifically for children by offering half-priced half portions, though most will provide reduced portions at reduced prices if you ask.

Florence

Obtaining Tickets

Tickets for most events can usually be obtained from the box office of the venue concerned. However, it can often be easier to use one of several commercial ticket agencies dotted around the city.

Information

Listings of current and forthcoming events can be obtained from the tourist office (which has lots of posters and pamphlets); from the pages of newspapers such as *La Nazione* and *La Repubblica*; and from listings magazines such as *Metro, Firenze Spettacolo, Time Off* and the English-language *Events*.

Classical Music

Florence's main classical music events take place during its big summer festivals (see below). During the rest of the year numerous smaller recitals of music are held in the city's churches and concert halls.

Amici della Musica

A group known as the Amici della Musica organises an October to April season of Saturday afternoon concerts (usually at the Teatro della Pergola).
✉ Via Sirtori 49 ☎ 055/608 420 or 607 440

Teatro della Pergola

✉ Via della Pergola 18, off Via Sant'Egidio ☎ 055/247 9651
🚌 6, 12, 14, 23, 71

Musicus Concernus

Another association, the Musicus Concernus, holds recitals between October and June at various city locations. A much used venue of theirs is the auditorium of the Palazzo dei Congressi.
✉ Piazza del Carmine 19 ☎ 055/287 347

Palazzo dei Congressi

✉ Viale F Strozzi (north of the railway station) ☎ No phone

Teatro Communale

The Teatro Comunale, the city's key performance venue, runs its own season of smaller concerts from September to mid-December, together with opera performances (Dec–Jan) and occasional symphony concerts (Jan–Apr).
✉ Corso Italia 16, off Lungarno Amerigo Vespucci ☎ 055/277 9236 🚌 Shuttle bus C

Teatro Verdi

The slightly smaller Teatro Verdi mixes opera and ballet productions with its theatrical repertoire between January and April
✉ Via Ghibellina 101 ☎ 055/239 6242 🚌 14

Santo Stefano

Another name to look out for is the Orchestra Regionale Toscana, which often presents chamber concerts in churches such as Santo Stefano.
✉ Via delle Pesce, off Via Por Santa Maria 🚌 None

Clubs, Discos and Live Music

Andromeda

A popular and very central club-disco which regularly changes its interior appearance to keep up with latest trends.
✉ Via dei Cimatori 13-Vicolo dei Cerchi ☎ 055/292 002 🕐 Closed Sun 🚌 In the pedestrian zone

Auditorium Flog

Currently the city's best-known and most important venue for live rock and jazz concerts. Hosts occasional one-off 'specials' devoted to particular musical genres. See listings for details.

✉ **Via Mercati 24b**
☎ **055/487 145** 🚌 **4**

Be-Bop

A long-established live jazz club housed in a suitably dive-like cellar. Very popular, particularly on Wednesday (usually the main night for live music), so arrive early to be sure of space.

✉ **Via dei Servi 28r** 🚌 **None**
🚌 **1, 6, 7, 10, 11 & services to Piazza San Marco**

Chiodo Fisso

This is a popular wine bar of long standing, known for its top quality folk concerts and also for occasional jazz concerts. The wine and snack food on offer are reliably good.

✉ **Via Dante Alighieri 16r**
☎ **055/238 1290** 🚌 **In the pedestrian zone**

Full Up

Many Florentine clubs and discos rise and fall quite quickly: this place has been around for some time, and is especially popular with a slightly older, more sophisticated crowd at the weekends.

✉ **Via della Vigna Vecchia 21, off Via del Proconsolo**
☎ **055/293 006** 🚌 **19**

Jazz Club

A club that plays jazz, as its name suggests, with serious music and appreciative audiences. You need to obtain membership to enter, but this is easily done at the door.

✉ **Via Nuova dei Caccini 3**
☎ **055/247 9700** 🚌 **6, 12, 14, 23, 71**

Maracanà

A lively Latin American disco housed in a former theatre, near to the railway station. You can eat a pizza looking down on the circular dance floor from the restaurant balcony. Maracanà also presents occasional, but very entertaining, Brazilian cabaret and floor-show.

✉ **Via Faenza 4** ☎ **055/210 298** 🚌 **All services to the railway station**

Meccanò

This is probably the most popular disco in Florence, although not the most central. Meccanò is situated some way to the west of the city centre by the Cascine park.

✉ **Piazza Vittorio Veneto**
☎ **055/31 371** 🕐 **Closed Mon**
🚌 **17c**

Space Electronic

This big central disco is much patronised by young summer visitors to the city. There is large dance floor upstairs and a quieter bar area downstairs for relaxing and talking.

✉ **Via Palazzuolo 37**
☎ **055/293 082** 🚌 **All services to the station**

Tenax

Tenax is the city's largest disco and it is popular with both visitors and Florentines alike. However, its peripheral position – out in the direction of the airport – means it is much more likely to appeal to dedicated clubbers only. Do give some advance thought as to how you will get home.

✉ **Via Pratese 46a, Peretola**
☎ **055/308 160** 🚌 **Best to take a taxi**

Ticket Agencies

The most central are: Box Office ✉ Via Faenza 139r ☎ 055/210 804; Agenzia Universalturismo ✉ Via Speziali 7r, between Piazza della Repubblica and Via dei Calzaiuoli ☎ 055/217 241; Agenzia Arno ✉ Piazza degli Ottaviani 7r, junction of Via dei Fossi and Via della Spada ☎ 055/219 512; Agenzia Globus ✉ Piazza Santa Trínita 2r ☎ 055/214 992.

Dance

National and international dance troupes tend to save their best for Florence's two big summer festivals, the Maggio Musicale Fiorentino and Estate Fiesolana (see main text). However, both the Teatro Comunale and Teatro della Pergola offer ballet performances as part of their regular seasons. Consult the tourist office for details of forthcoming events.

Music Festivals

Maggio Musicale Fiorentino

Florence's premier cultural event is the Maggio Musicale Fiorentino, an internationally renowned festival of opera and classical music held between late April and early July. The festival has its own orchestra, chorus and ballet troupe, but alternates its house companies with guest appearances by visiting international orchestras and choirs. Most of the larger events are staged at the Teatro Comunale, which also serves as the festival's main box office (you are advised to book as early as possible), or at the Teatro Piccolo (or Ridotto), the Comunale's smaller auditorium. Other popular venues for smaller works include the Teatro della Pergola (see Classical Music for details), the Palazzo dei Congressi (see Classical Music for details), Teatro Verdi and Giardino dei Boboli.

Estate Fiesolana

The city's other big music festival is the Estate Fiesolana, a summer season of concerts held between late June and August. Like the Maggio Musicale it also offers peripheral opera, ballet, theatre and film presentations. Many of the concerts take place in attractive Fiesole in the hills above the city, where the old Teatro Romano (Roman theatre) provides a striking and escapist venue for a series of outdoor evening recitals. Other performances take place in the Badia

Fiesolana near by, or in Florence at a number of different locations such as Santa Croce and Palazzo Pitti.

Estate Fiesolana (Box Office)
✉ Via Faenza 139 ☎ 055/210 804

Palazzo dei Congressi
✉ Viale F Strozzi (north of the railway station) ☎ No phone

Teatro Comunale
✉ Corso Italia 16, off Lungarno Amerigo Vespucci ☎ 055/277 9236 🚌 Shuttle bus C

Teatro della Pergola
✉ Via della Pergola 18, off Via Sant'Egidio ☎ 055/247 9651
🚌 6, 12, 14, 23, 71

Teatro Verdi
✉ Via Ghibellina 101
☎ 055/239 6242 🚌 14

Theatre

Virtually all of the Florentine theatrical productions staged will be beyond anyone without a good grasp of Italian. If you do want to see a production, however, the city's leading theatres are the Teatro della Pergola, which presents mainstream classical plays performed by leading Italian companies; the similar Teatro Verdi (see Music Festivals for details); and for something quite different the Teatro Niccolini, which is one of the city's oldest theatres, yet now offers a good mixture of classic modern and ground-breaking contemporary works.

Teatro Niccolini
(✉ Via Ricasoli 3
☎ 055/213 282).

Tuscany

Classical Music

Accademia Musicale Chigiana

Tuscany in the summer offers a wealth of small-town cultural festivals. One of the most prestigious belongs to Siena, where the Settimana Musicale Senese in July sees a week of performances by the acclaimed Accademia Musicale Chigiana.

🖂 Via di Città 89, Siena
☎ 0577/46 152 🕓 Jul

Festival Pucciniano

Equally well-known is the Festival Pucciniano, a series of outdoor concerts of Puccini's music held in August at Torre del Lago (near Lucca). Lucca itself stages the major Sagra Musicale Lucchese, a wide-ranging summer arts festival.

🖂 Fondazione Festival Pucciniano, Torre del Lago ☎ Information: 0584/359 322. Box office: 0584/350 567 🕓 Aug

Cantiere Internazionale d'Arte

Montepulciano's Cantiere Internazionale d'Arte (August) concentrates on new or more avante-garde works by composers, dramatists and choreographers. If you are unable to attend these larger festivals, enquire at tourist offices or keep your eyes open for posters advertising small church or other year-round recitals.

🖂 Montepulciano
☎ Tourist office: 0578/758 687 or 757 442 🕓 Aug

San Gimignano

Slightly less exalted than the Festival Pucciniano or the Settimana Musicale Senese, but more varied and intimate, is the San Gimignano festival (in July), which has been held in the village virtually every year since the 1920s. It offers a wide range of music, film and theatrical presentations, usually culminating in two gala opera performances outdoors in the Piazza del Duomo. As with many of the festivals, book early (ideally before starting your holiday) to avoid disappointment.

🖂 Piazza del Duomo 1
☎ 0577/940 008 🕓 Jul

Clubs and Discos

Nightlife of the clubs and disco variety, whether for teenagers or a sophisticated older crowd, is in very short supply in most of Tuscany's somnolent little hill towns. Exceptions include Siena, where there are a few clubs (situated mostly in the suburbs of the city), and occasional discos in and around Lucca, Pisa and Colle di Val d'Elsa (see up-to-date listings in *La Nazione*, Tuscany's local newspaper, for further details and locations).

There are also plenty of bars and clubs along the Versilia coast (north of Lucca), whose string of beach resorts play host to thousands of young summer visitors in search of night-time action.

One of the most popular towns is Viareggio, thanks mainly to the fact it can be easily reached from Florence in around an hour. Many Florentines spend their summer nights in the town's many bars, nightclubs and seafood restaurants. Another more up-market town with plenty of nightlife is Forte dei Marmi.

Something Different in Siena

The bi-annual bareback horserace around the Piazza del Campo is unmissable if the timing of your visit coincides with the Palio (▶ panel 116).

What's On When

The Palio

The most famous event in the Tuscan year is the Palio, a bi-annual bareback horserace around the Piazza del Campo in Siena. Run virtually every year since medieval times, it takes its name from the *pallium*, or banner, awarded to the winner. Contestants are drawn from each of Siena's 17 *contrade*, or parishes, though only ten are represented in the race (lots are drawn to choose the ten). Competition is fierce – the race is far more than a tourist spectacle – as loyalty to the *contrade* is intense. Each has its own flag, heraldic motif (usually animal), as well as its own church, museum and social centre. Drummers and flag-tossers from each also parade in the orgy of processions and ceremonies that precede each Palio. The race lasts only 90 seconds, but celebrations can go on for weeks. If you can't be in Siena on race day, national television usually broadcasts the event live.

January

Pitti Immagine: Florence fashion shows.

February

Carnival celebrations across Tuscany, notably processions in Viareggio and San Gimignano (Shrove Tuesday and adjacent weekends).

March

Festa dell'Annunziata: fair in Florence's Piazza Santissima Annunziata (25th).

April

Lucca's summer Sagra Musicale (Music Festival) begins.
Holy Week celebrations many towns and villages
Mostra dell'Artigianato (Florence): international exhibition of crafts and artisans' work (last week).
Scoppio del Carro (Explosion of the Cart): Easter Sunday service in Florence's Duomo followed by special fireworks.

May

Festa del Grillo: crickets are sold and released in Florence's Cascine park (Sun after Ascension).
Maggio Musicale (Florence): international festival of music and dance.
Pisa's 'Historic Regatta of the Maritime Republics' (May–Jun).

June

Start of summer arts and music festival in San Gimignano.
Luminaria di San Ranieri: fireworks and illuminated streets in Pisa followed the next day by a historic regatta.
Calcio in Costume: medieval football match in Florence *Il Gioco del Ponte*: Pisa's

costumed 'Battle of the Bridge' (last Sun).
Estate Fiesolana: arts and musical festival in Fiesole.

July

Corso del Palio: world-famous horse race in Siena's main square (2nd).
Festa di San Paolino (Lucca): crossbow contest and procession.
Opera festival at Barga near Lucca (second half).

August

Cantiere Internazionale (Montepulciano): festival of contemporary music and dance (first half).
Montepulciano food festival (second Sun).
Corso del Palio: second horse race in Siena's main square
Luminaria di Santa Croce (Lucca): torchlit procession
Bravio delle Botti (Montepulciano): barrel-rolling contest through the streets (last Sun).
International festival of choral music in Arezzo (last two weeks).
Festival Pucciniano: month-long outdoor festival of Puccini's music at Torre del Lago (near Lucca).
Settimana Musicale Senese: week-long music festival in Siena (last week).

September

Festa delle Rificolone (Florence): torchlit procession
Giostro del Saracino (Arezzo): jousting contest in medieval costume (first Sun).
Wine festivals across the region, notably Greve.

October

Florence opera and classical music season, the Teatro Comunale.

Practical
Matters

GMT 12 noon	Italy 1PM	Germany 1PM	USA (NY) 7AM	Netherlands 1PM	Spain 1PM
→	→	←	→	→	

BEFORE YOU GO

WHAT YOU NEED

		UK	Germany	USA	Netherlands	Spain
●	Required					
○	Suggested					
▲	Not required					
Passport		●	●	●	●	●
Visa		▲	▲	▲	▲	▲
Onward or Return Ticket		▲	▲	▲	▲	▲
Health Inoculations		▲	▲	▲	▲	▲
Health Documentation (► 123, Health)		●	●	▲	●	●
Travel Insurance		○	○	○	○	○
Driving Licence (national)		●	●	●	●	●
Car Insurance Certificate (if own car)		○	○	○	○	○
Car Registration Document (if own car)		●	●	●	●	●

WHEN TO GO

Florence

- ▬▬▬ High season
- ▭ Low season

JAN	FEB	MAR	APR	MAY	JUN	JUL	AUG	SEP	OCT	NOV	DEC
6°C	6°C	10°C	13°C	17°C	22°C	25°C	25°C	21°C	16°C	11°C	6°C

Very wet   Wet   Cloud   Sun

TOURIST OFFICES

In the UK
Italian State Tourist Board
1 Princes Street
London W1R 8AY
☎ 0171 408 1254
Fax: 0171 493 6695

In the USA
Italian Government Travel
Office (ENIT)
630 Fifth Avenue
Suite 1565
New York NY 10111
☎ 212/245 4822
Fax: 212/586 9249

Italian Government Travel
Office (ENIT)
12400 Wilshire Boulevard
Suite 550
Los Angeles, CA 90025
☎ 310/820 1898
Fax: 310/820 6357

POLICE 112

FIRE 115

AMBULANCE 113

ROAD ASSISTANCE (ACI) 116

WHEN YOU ARE THERE

ARRIVING

The main entry into Tuscany is Pisa (Galileo Galilei) Airport (☎ 050/500707), though there are charter flights landing at Perètola, close to Florence (☎ 055/373498). There is a direct rail link between Florence and Pisa Airport (journey time, 1 hour).

Pisa (Galileo Galilei) Airport
Kilometres to city centre   **Journey times**

2 kilometres

🚇	5 minutes
🚌	4 minutes
🚗	30 minutes

Florence Perètola (Amerigo Vespucci) Airport
Kilometres to city centre   **Journey times**

5 kilometres

🚇	N/A
🚌	10 minutes
🚗	30 minutes

MONEY

The monetary unit of Italy is the Italian Lira (plural: Lire), which is abbreviated to Lit or L. Tourists must get used to counting in thousands and millions as the denominations are: coins of 5, 10, 20, 50, 100, 200 and 500 Lire and notes of 1,000, 2,000, 5,000, 10,000, 50,000 and 100,000 Lire. There are plans to introduce a 'new Lira' worth 1,000 times the present currency.

TIME

 Italy is one hour ahead of Greenwich Mean Time (GMT+1), but from late March, when clocks are put forward one hour, to late September, Italian Summer Time (GMT+2) operates.

CUSTOMS

→ **YES**

Goods Obtained Duty Free Inside the EU or Goods Bought Outside the EU (Limits):
Alcohol (over 22° vol): 1L **or** Alcohol (not over 22° vol): 2L **or** Wine: 2L **and** Still table wine: 2L
Cigarettes: 200 **or** Cigarillos: 100 **or** Cigars: 50 **or** Tobacco: 250gms
Perfume: 60ml
Toilet Water: 250ml
Goods Bought Duty Free and Tax Paid Inside the EU (Guidance Levels):
Alcohol (over 22° vol) : 10L
Alcohol (not over 22° vol) : 20L
Wine (max 60L sparkling: 90L
Beer: 110L
Cigarettes: 800 **or** Cigarillos: 400 **or** Cigars: 200 **or** Tobacco: 1kg
Perfume/Toilet Water: no limit
(You must be 17 and over to benefit from the alcohol and tobacco allowances.)

➖ **NO**

Drugs, firearms, ammunition, offensive weapons, obscene material, unlicensed animals.

CONSULATES

UK	Germany	USA	Netherlands	Spain
055/284133	055/294722	055/2398276	055/475249	055/217110
(Florence)	(Florence)	(Florence)	(Florence)	(Florence)

WHEN YOU ARE THERE

TOURIST OFFICES

Tuscany Regional Tourist Board

● Via di Novoli 26
50127 Firenze (Florence)
☎ 055/4383111
Fax: 055/4383064

Florence Tourist Office

● Via Cavour
Firenze (Florence)
☎ 055/290832

Other Tourist Offices

● Piazza Risorgimento 116
Arezzo, ☎ 0575/23952

● Via Nazionale 70
Visitors & Convention
Cortona, ☎ 0575/630357

● Piazza Guidiccioni 2
Lucca, ☎ 0583/491205

● Piazza Duomo
Pisa, ☎ 050/560464

● Piazza del Duomo
Pistóia, ☎ 0573/21622

● Via Muzzi 51
Prato, ☎ 0574/35141

● Piazza Duomo
San Gimignano
☎ 0577/940008

● Piazza del Campo 56
Siena, ☎ 0577/280551

● Viale G Carducci 10
Viareggio, ☎ 0574/35141

NATIONAL HOLIDAYS

J	F	M	A	M	J	J	A	S	O	N	D
2		1	2	1			1			1	4

1 Jan	New Year's Day
6 Jan	Epiphany
Mar/Apr	Easter Sunday and Monday
25 Apr	Liberation Day, 1945
1 May	Labour Day
15 Aug	Assumption of the Virgin
1 Nov	All Saints' Day
8 Dec	Immaculate Conception
25 Dec	Christmas Day
26 Dec	St Stephen's Day
25 Dec	Christmas Day

Banks, businesses and most shops and museums are closed on these days. Florence celebrates its patron saint (St John the Baptist) on 24 June, but most places stay open.

OPENING HOURS

○ Shops	● Attractions/museums
● Offices	● Post offices
● Banks	● Pharmacies

9AM	10AM	11AM	12PM	2PM	3PM	4PM	5PM	6PM

☐ Day	☐ Mid day
☐ Evening	

In addition to the times shown above, afternoon opening times of shops in winter is 3 to 6PM. Department stores and shops in tourist areas may remain open all day and sometimes, until later in the evening. Some shops are closed Monday morning, others on Saturday afternoon or all day Saturday. Nearly all shops close Sunday. Bank afternoon opening times vary but all are closed weekends. Museum times also vary – smaller museums tend to open only in the morning (9AM to 1/2PM) and have restricted winter hours. Museums often close early on Sunday (around noon) and most close Mondays.

DRIVE ON THE
RIGHT

TOILETS
CHARGE

PUBLIC TRANSPORT

Internal Flights Services throughout the country are provided by Alitalia – the national airline (☎ 06-65641), and its associated companies ATI (☎ 081-7091111) and Avianova (☎ 06-6551617). The flight time to Florence from Rome is 75 minutes; and from Milan 60 minutes.

Trains Italian State Railways (Ferrovie dello Stato, or FS) provide a well-run and inexpensive service. Florence is the hub of the Tuscan rail network with good connections with Pisa, Arrezo, Lucca and Viaréggio. The train is more comfortable than a bus but generally less frequent. There are two classes of travel: first and second.

Regional Buses There is no national bus company, though Lazzi (☎ 055-363041) and SITA (☎ 055-278611) both have a major presence in Tuscany. Bus terminals in larger towns are often next to the railway station; in smaller towns and villages most buses pull in at the central piazza.

Ferries Tuscany has three ferry ports: Livorno serves Corsica, Sardinia, Sicily and the Tuscan Archipelago. Piombino has services to Elba, connecting to Portoferraio and Corsica plus the smaller ports of Cavo and Rio Marina. Porto Santo Stefano has ferries to Corsica and the island of Giglio.

Urban Transport City buses are cheap charging a flat fare. Invariably you need a ticket before getting on. Buy them in a tabacchi or from kiosks at bus terminals and stops. In Florence most routes pass by the station. The service is reasonably frequent but buses can get very crowded in rush hours.

CAR RENTAL

Car hire is available in most cities and resorts from international and Italian companies, but is not cheap. Generally small local firms offer better rates but cars can only be booked locally. Air or train travellers can take advantage of special inclusive deals.

TAXIS

Taxis are available in all towns and tourist resorts. Taxis can be hailed, though you will be lucky to find one passing when you want one. Otherwise find a taxi rank (usually at stations and major piazze), or call a radio taxi (in Florence, ☎ 055-4390 or 055-4798)..

DRIVING

Speed limits on motorways (autostrade), for which there are tolls: **130kph**

Speed limits on main roads: **110kph**; secondary roads: **90kph**

Speed limits on urban roads: **50kph**

Must be worn in front seats at all times and in rear seats where fitted.

Random breath-testing is frequent. Limit: 80mg per 100ml blood.

Petrol is more expensive in Italy than in Britain and most other European countries. If bringing your own car you are entitled to petrol coupons (15 per cent off). All except garages in rural places sell unleaded petrol (*senza piombo*). Outside urban areas petrol stations open 7AM to 12.30PM and 3 to 7.30pm. Credit cards are rarely accepted.

In the event of a breakdown, ring 116, giving your registration number and type of car and the nearest ACI (Automobile Club d'Italia) office will assist you. You will be towed to the nearest ACI garage. This service is free to foreign-registered vehicles or cars rented from Rome or Milan airport (you will need to produce your passport).

PERSONAL SAFETY

The *Carabinieri* (military-style) uniforms and white shoulder belts) deal with general crime and public order. Tuscans are law-abiding. Petty theft is the main problem (bag-snatching, pickpocketing and car break-ins). Some precautions:

- Carry shoulder bags not *on* your shoulder but slung *across* your body.
- Scooter-borne bag-snatchers can be foiled if you keep on the inside of the pavement.
- Do not put anything down on a café or restaurant table.
- Lock car doors and never keep valuables in your car.

Police assistance:
☎ **112**
from any call box

TELEPHONES

Almost every bar in Italy has a telephone, plus many in public places. They take 100, 200 or 500 Lire coins, or tokens (gettoni) worth 200 Lire, and more often phone-cards (schede telefoniche) valued 5,000 and 10,000 Lire. Tokens and phonecards are available from SIP (state telephone company) offices, tobacconists, stations and other public places.

International Dialling Codes
From Italy to:

UK:	**00 44**
Germany:	**00 49**
USA:	**00 1**
Netherlands:	**00 31**
Spain:	**00 34**

POST

Post Offices
The Italian postal system is notoriously slow. In Florence the central post office is in Via Pellicceria. Post offices in cities and major towns open 8AM to 6PM (12.30PM Saturday), other offices: Open: 8AM to 1.30/2PM (11.45AM Sat). Closed: Sun
☎ 055/214145

ELECTRICITY

The power supply is:
220 volts

Type of socket: Round two- or three-hole sockets taking plugs of two round pins or sometimes three pins in a vertical row. British visitors should bring an adaptor; US visitors a voltage transformer.

TIPS/GRATUITIES

Yes ✓ No ✗		
Hotels (if service not included)	✓	10–15%
Restaurants (if service not included)	✓	10–15%
Cafés/Bars	✓	L100 min
Taxis	✗	
Porters	✓	L2.000
Chambermaids	✓	L3.000/week
Usherettes	✓	L1.000
Hairdressers	✓	L3.000 min
Cloakroom attendants	✓	L1.000
Toilets	✓	L100

PHOTOGRAPHY
Light: Tuscany is noted for its soft light compared to the brighter light of the south and the hazier light of the north of the country.
Where you can photograph: Most museums and certain churches will not allow you to photograph inside; check first.
Film and developing: A roll of film is called a *pellicola*, but 'film' should get you understood. Film and developing are much more expensive in Italy than in the UK or USA.

HEALTH

Insurance
Nationals of EU countries receive free medical treatment and pay a percentage of prescribed medicines. Hospital treatment is at reduced cost. You need a qualifying document (Form E111 for Britons). However, private medical insurance is advised for all.

Dental Services
Nationals of EU countries can obtain dental treatment at reduced cost at dentists which operate within the Italian health service. A qualifying document (Form E111 for Britons) is needed. Still, private medical insurance is advised for all.

Sun Advice
In summer, particularly in July and August, it can get very near hot on the coast and low-lying land. You can get sunburnt surprisingly quickly, even through cloud, so a sunscreen is recommended at all times.

Drugs
Pharmacies (*farmacia*), recognised by their green cross sign, possess highly trained staff able to offer medical advice on minor ailments and provide a wide range of prescribed and non-prescribed medicines and drugs.

Safe Water
It is quite safe to drink tap water and water from drinking fountains, but never drink from a tap marked *acqua non potabile*. However, many Italians prefer the taste of bottled mineral which is widely available.

CONCESSIONS

Students/Youths Holders of an International Student Identity Card (ISIC) can take advantage of discounts offered to travelling students. Those under 26 that are not students can obtain an International Youth Card from student organisations that entitles the holder to discounts on transport, accommodation, museums.

Senior Citizens Citizens aged over 60 of EU and a number of other countries with which Italy has a reciprocal arrangement (not including USA) may gain free admission to communal and state museums and receive discounts at other museums and on public transport on production of their passport.

CLOTHING SIZES

Italy	UK	Rest of Europe	USA	
46	36	46	36	Suits
48	38	48	38	Suits
50	40	50	40	Suits
52	42	52	42	Suits
54	44	54	44	Suits
56	46	56	46	Suits
41	7	41	8	Shoes
42	7.5	42	8.5	Shoes
43	8.5	43	9.5	Shoes
44	9.5	44	10.5	Shoes
45	10.5	45	11.5	Shoes
46	11	46	12	Shoes
37	14.5	37	14.5	Shirts
38	15	38	15	Shirts
39/40	15.5	39/40	15.5	Shirts
41	16	41	16	Shirts
42	16.5	42	16.5	Shirts
43	17	43	17	Shirts
38	8	34	6	Dresses
40	10	36	8	Dresses
42	12	38	10	Dresses
44	14	40	12	Dresses
46	16	42	14	Dresses
48	18	44	16	Dresses
38	4.5	38	6	Shoes
38	5	38	6.5	Shoes
39	5.5	39	7	Shoes
39	6	39	7.5	Shoes
40	6.5	40	8	Shoes
41	7	41	8.5	Shoes

WHEN DEPARTING

- Contact the airport or airline the day prior to leaving to ensure flight details are unchanged.
- The airport departure tax, payable when you leave Italy, is included in the cost of the airline ticket.
- Check the duty-free limits of the country you are entering before departure.

LANGUAGE

Italian is the native language. The Tuscan dialect is the purest form of spoken Italian. Many Italians speak English but you will be better received if you at least attempt to communicate in Italian. Italian words are pronounced phonetically. Every vowel and consonant (except 'h') is sounded. The accent usually (but not always) falls on the penultimate syllable.

Below is a list of a few words that may be helpful. More extensive coverage can be found in the AA's *Essential Italian Phrase Book* which lists 2,000 phrases and 2,000 words.

hotel	*albergo*	toilet	*toilette*
room	*camera*	bath	*bagno*
..single/double	*..singola/doppia*	shower	*doccia*
..one/two nights	*..per una/due notte/i*	balcony	*balcone*
..per person/per room	*..per una/due persona/e*	reception	*reception*
		key	*chiave*
reservation	*prenotazione*	room service	*servizio da camera*
rate	*tariffa*		
breakfast	*prima colazione*	chambermaid	*cameriera*

bank	*banco*	banknote	*banconota*
exchange office	*cambio*	coin	*moneta*
post office	*posta*	credit card	*carta di credito*
cashier	*cassiere/a*	traveller's cheque	*assegno turistico*
foreign exchange	*cambio con l'estero*	commission charge	*commissione*
foreign currency	*valuta estera*	cheque book	*libretto degli assegni*
pound sterling	*sterlina*		
American dollar	*dollaro*	exchange rate	*tasso di cambio*

restaurant	*ristorante*	starter	*il primo*
café	*caffè*	main course	*il secondo*
table	*tavolo*	dish of the day	*piatto del giorno*
menu	*menù/carta*	dessert	*dolci*
set menu	*menù/turistico*	drink	*bevanda*
wine list	*lista dei vini*	waiter	*cameriere*
lunch	*pranzo/colazione*	waitress	*cameriera*
dinner	*cena*	the bill	*conto*

aeroplane	*aeroplano*	..single/return	*..andata sola/ andata e ritorno*
airport	*aeroporto*		
train	*treno*		
..station	*stazione ferroviaria*	..first/second class	*..prima/seconda classe*
bus	*autobus*	ticket office	*biglietteria*
..station	*autostazione*	timetable	*orario*
ferry	*traghetto*	seat	*posto*
..terminal	*stazione maríttima*	non-smoking	*vietato fumare*
ticket	*biglietto*	reserved	*prenotato*

yes	*sì*	help!	*aiuto!*
no	*no*	today	*oggi*
please	*per favore*	tomorrow	*domani*
thank you	*grazie*	yesterday	*ieri*
hello	*ciao*	how much?	*quanto?*
goodbye	*arrivederci*	expensive	*caro*
goodnight	*buona notte*	open	*aperto*
sorry	*mi dispiace*	closed	*chiuso*

INDEX

Acknowledgements
The Automobile Association wishes to thank the following libraries, photographers and associations for their assistance in the preparation of this book:

THE BRIDGEMAN ART LIBRARY, LONDON 34b general view of the Chapel by Masolino and Filippino Lippi Masaccio (15th c.) Brancacci Chapel, Santa Maria del Carmine, Florence; 35b Battle of the Centaurs, relief by Michelangelo Buonarroti (1475–1564) (marble) Casa Buonarroti, Florence; 49b Pitti Palace: Vault of the Sala de Giove, paintings by Pietro da Cortona and Ciro Ferri, 1643
MRI BANKERS' GUIDE TO FOREIGN CURRENCY 119
SCALA 38b Giardino di Boboli, Florence
SPECTRUM COLOUR LIBRARY 61

The remaining pictures are from the Association's own library (AA PHOTO LIBRARY) and were taken by C Sawyer with the exception of the following: J Edmanson 5b, 11b, 40b, 46b, 50, 55b, 86, 122c; K Paterson F/Cover (a), 1, 2, 6b, 7b, 9b, 10b, 12b, 19b, 21, 22b, 27a, 43b, 59b, 67, 70a, 71, 72a, 72b, 73a, 74a, 75, 76a, 77, 78, 79a, 79b, 80, 80/1, 82, 83a, 83b, 84, 85a, 88, 89, 90, 91b, 117b; B Smith 27b, 31b, 54/5, 62b, 91a, 92, 93, 94, 95, 96, 97, 98, 99, 100, 101, 102, 103, 104, 105, 106, 107, 108, 109, 110, 111, 112, 113, 114, 115, 116, 122a; T Souter 56b; W Voysey B/Cover, 117a.

Author's Acknowledgements Tim Jepson wishes to thank his editor and Duncan and Amanda Baird.

Contributors
Copy editor: Nia Williams Page Layout: Design 23 Verifier: Teresa Fisher
Researcher (Practical Matters): Colin Follett Indexer: Marie Lorimer

Dear Essential Traveller

Your comments, opinions and recommendations are very important to us. So please help us to improve our travel guides by taking a few minutes to complete this simple questionnaire.

You do not need a stamp (unless posted outside the UK). If you do not want to cut this page from your guide, then photocopy it or write your answers on a plain sheet of paper.

Send to: **The Editor, AA World Travel Guides, FREEPOST SCE 4598, Basingstoke RG21 4GY.**

Your recommendations...

We always encourage readers' recommendations for restaurants, nightlife or shopping – if your recommendation is used in the next edition of the guide, we will send you a *FREE* AA *Essential* **Guide** of your choice. Please state below the establishment name, location and your reasons for recommending it.

_____
_____
_____
_____

Please send me **AA *Essential*** _____
(*see list of titles inside the front cover*)

About this guide...

Which title did you buy?
AA *Essential* _____
Where did you buy it? _____
When? m m / y y

Why did you choose an AA *Essential* Guide? _____
_____
_____
_____
_____

Did this guide meet your expectations?
Exceeded ☐ Met all ☐ Met most ☐ Fell below ☐
Please give your reasons _____
_____
_____
_____

continued on next page...

Were there any aspects of this guide that you particularly liked? _____

_____

_____

_____

Is there anything we could have done better? _____

_____

_____

_____

_____

About you…

Name (*Mr/Mrs/Ms*) _____

    Address _____

    _____

    _____ Postcode _____

    Daytime tel nos _____

Which age group are you in?

    Under 25 ☐ 25–34 ☐ 35–44 ☐ 45–54 ☐ 55–64 ☐ 65+ ☐

How many trips do you make a year?

    Less than one ☐ One ☐ Two ☐ Three or more ☐

Are you an AA member? Yes ☐ No ☐

About your trip…

When did you book? m m / y y   When did you travel? m m / y y

How long did you stay? _____

Was it for business or leisure? _____

Did you buy any other travel guides for your trip?

    If yes, which ones? _____

    _____

Thank you for taking the time to complete this questionnaire. Please send
it to us as soon as possible, and remember, you do not need a stamp
(*unless posted outside the UK*).

Happy Holidays!